B Powell

The guide to preferment

or Powell's complete book of cookery

B Powell

The guide to preferment
or Powell's complete book of cookery

ISBN/EAN: 9783742811943

Manufactured in Europe, USA, Canada, Australia, Japa

Cover: Foto ©Gila Hanssen / pixelio.de

Manufactured and distributed by brebook publishing software (www.brebook.com)

B Powell

The guide to preferment

A Complete INDEX,

For the Immediate finding what is wanted.

Roasting in General.   Page
FOR roasting Beef   9
For roasting Mutton   10
To roast a Shoulder of Mutton with Thyme   11
For roasting a Leg of Mutton with Cockles
To roast a Leg or Shoulder of Mutton with Oysters
To roll a Breast of Mutton   12
To roast a Chine of Mutton
For roasting Mutton, Venison Fashion
For roasting Veal   13
An admirable Way to roast a Calf's Head
Lamb or Veal   14
For roasting Calf's Liver
For roasting a Pig
For roasting Pork   15

Roasting of Poultry.
For roasting a Capon
Pullets with Eggs or without
Chickens
For roasting a Turkey   17
For roasting a Goose   18
How to truss a Goose   19
For roasting a Woodcock
Another Way for roasting Larks

To roast a Wild Duck   20
How to truss Easterlings, Ducks, Teals and Widgeons
A good Sauce for Teal, Mallard, Ducks, &c.   21
For roasting a Hare
How to truss a Hare   22
For roasting Rabbits   23
French Sauce for Rabbits
How to truss a Rabbit for roasting
For roasting a Haunch of Venison   24
To roast Tripe
To roast a Tongue and Udder   25
Roasting a pickled Neat's Tongue
To roast Lobsters
To roast a Pike   26

Instructions for Boiling.
Boiling Beef   27
To boil Mutton
boil a Leg of Mutton with Stuffing   28
boil Veal
For boiling a Leg of Lamb with the Loin fried about it

THE

	Page		Page
A Leg of Lamb boiled, with Chickens round it		To boil Pike	
To boil pickled Pork	29	boil fresh Cod	38
For keeping Meat hot		boil barrel Cod, or or any other salt Fish	
To boil Greens			
For boiling Sprouts and Cabbage		boil a Cod's Head	
To dress Spinage	30	bail a Jowl of Salmon	39
For boiling Carrots		make an excellent Sauce for Salmon	
boiling Cauliflowers		boil a Turburt, or Holiburt	
boiling Brockala			
boiling French Beans	31	*Broiling.*	
boiling Asparagus		To broil Chickens	40
boiling Artichokes		To broil Sheep or Hog's Tongues	41
Boiling Poultry.		For broiling Beef Steaks	
To boil Pullets and Oysters	32	To broil Fish	
To boil Fowls		To broil Chubs	
To dress Chickens and Asparagus		For broiling Whitings	42
For boiling Chickens		For broiling Cod-founds	
For making Sauce to the Chickens	33	*Frying.*	
To boil a Turkey with Oysters		How to fry Beaf-steaks	43
		To fry Beaf-steaks with Oysters	
For boiling a Turkey	34	How to fry Mutton-steaks	44
For making Stuffing for a boiled Turkey		For frying Veal-cutlets	
For making Sauce to a boiled Turkey		Frying Calves Feet in Butter	45
To boil Pidgeons	35	To fry a Quarter of Lamb	
To boil Ducks		How to fry Oysters	
For boiling a Goose		How to fry Pancakes	46
To boil Geese		How to make apple Fretters	
For boiling Rabbits	36	For making an apple Tansey	
Boiling Rabbits with Sausages		For making a gooseberry Tansey	
For boiling a Ham			
To boil a Tongue		For making a water Tansey	47
Boiling Fish.		For making apple Froise	
To boil a Salmon	37	To fry Eals	48

INDEX.

	Page
Fricaseys in General.	
For making a Fricasey of Chickens	
For making a brown Fricasey of Chickens	49
For fricaseying Calves Feet white	50
A white Fricasey of Chickens	
How to fricasey Ducks	
For Fricaseying a Goose	51
To fricasey Pidgeons in their Blood	
To fricasey Chickens and Rabbits	52
For making a brown Fricasey of Rabbits	
For making a white Fricasey of Rabbits	
How to fricasey cold roast Beef	63
To fricasey Veal	
To make a Fricasey of Lamb	54
Fricasey of Eggs	
Directions for Hashing.	
For hashing a Calves Head	55
For hashing Beef	56
To hash Chickens	
For hashing a Leg of Mutton	
For hashing any Part of Mutton	57
Directions for Stewing.	
An exceeding good Way to stew Chickens	
For stewing Ducks whole	58
To stew wild Fowl	
To stew a green Goose	
For stewing Pidgeons	59
To stew Pidgeons white	
Giblets stew'd	
For stewing Rabbits	90
For stewing a Pig	
For stewing Beef	
For stewing a Rump of Beef	61
For stewing Beef Collops	
To stew Beaf Steaks	92
To stew a Neck, Breast, Knuckle, or any other Joint of Veal	
For stewing Veal	63
To stew a Neck or Breast of Mutton	
For stewing a Rump or Leg of Mutton	94
For stewing Mutton Chops	
To stew Sausages	
For stewing a Carp	
For stewing Trout	
For stewing Cod	65
To stew Crabs	
For stewing Oysters	
For stewing Pike	66
To stew Tench	
To stew Carp an admirable Way	67
To butter Lobsters	
To stew a Pike with Oysters	
A Pudding for the Belly of a Pike	68
To dress Smelts	
To make a good Sauce for all fresh Fish	
How to clean and dress a Turtle	
To stew Snipes	69
A Ragoo of Snipes	
Force Meats.	
Forc'd Meats to be used as Occasion requires	70

THE

	Page		Page
To make Forc'd meat Balls		Beef dry'd after the Yorkshire Way.	
Chickens forc'd with Oysters	71	To make Muſtard Eggs made to eat Muſhroom	82
An exceeding Way of dreſſing Chickens		To make Solomongunda To make Sauſages	
Of Potting.		Sauſages of Veal or Lamb	83
To pot Beef	72	Veal or Mutton Cutlets	
For potting a Hare		To make Polonia Sauſages	
For potting Tongues	73		
Another Way		melt Butter, and reſtore it when oyl'd	
For potting Mutton			
For potting Cheſhire Cheeſe	74	clariſy Butter	84
		Parſley and Butter	
For making white Scotch Collops		To make good Gravy	85
Scotch Collops an excellent Way		Directions concerning Garden Things	
Of Ragoos.		*Of Soups, Broths and Gravy.*	
For ragooing Lamb Stones	75		
For ragooing a Breaſt of Veal		To make Broths for Soups or Gravy	86
A Ragoo of Cock's-combs, Cock's-kidneys and fat Livers	76	make a fine white Soup	
		make Solid, or portable Soup	
For dreſſing Lamb in ragoo		make Peaſe Soup	87
Of Collaring.		Vermicelly Soup	
For collaring Beef	77	Cellery Soup	98
For collaring a Breaſt of Veal		Onion Soup	
		Of gravy Soup	
For collaring Mutton		For making a Calves Head Soup	89
For collaring Pork	78		
For collaring Pig		Rice Soup	
For collaring Eals		A good Engliſh Soup	
Salting, Drying, &c.		Beef Broth	
To ſalt Hams, Tongues &c.	79	Mutton Broth	90
A Leg of Pork Ham Faſhion	80	For making jelly Broth, for conſumptive Perſons	
To dry Hams		A ſtrong Broth	
To dry Neat's Tongues to be dry'd	81	Fine Gravy	91

INDEX.

Baking.
	Page
For baking Beef the French Way.	
To bake Beef like red Deer	
For baking a Calves Head	92
For baking Herrings	
For making Ginger-bread	93

Directions to make Pies and Pasties.
	Page
Puff Paste	
Paste for a high Pie	
A Lear for Pasties	94
For making minc'd Pies	
For making a savory Chicken Pie	
A Pidgeon Pie	95
How to make a Turkey Pie	
For making a Goose Pie	
How to make a young Rook Pie	
A good common Crust for large Pies	
A standing Crust for large Pies of any Sort	97
A good Crust with cold Water	
A good Crust with Beef Dripping	
For making a Giblet Pie	
For making a Venison Pasty	98
Beef Pasty	
How to make a Hare Pie	
How to make a Rabbit Pie	
A Lamb Stone or Sweetbread Pie	99
For making a Mutton Pie	
How to make a Pork Pie	100
A Pork Pie for eating cold	
Veal Pie to be eat cold	
The best Ingredients for sweet Pies	101
The Ingredients for savory Pies	
To make puff Paste for Pies	
For Paste Royal	
To make a Crust for a raised Pie	102
A fine Paste for patty Pans	
How to make an Apple Pie	
To make very good Whigs	
How to make an Artichoke Pie	103
For making a Potatoe Pie	
How to make a Herring Pie	
For making an Eal Pie	104
To make an Oyster Pie	
To make a Trout Pie	
To make a Tench Pie	

Of Tarts.
	Page
To ice Tarts	105
A short Paste for Tarts	
To make a Gooseberry Tart	
To make a Cherry Tart	106
To make black Tart Stuff	
To make yellow Tart Stuff	
A proper Paste for Tarts	

Puddings.
	Page
For making a very fine Pudding	107
A very good Plumb Pudding and not expensive	108
For making a bailed Plumb Pudding	
For making a Bread Pudding	

THE

	Page		Page
For making an Apple Pudding		How to make a light Seed Cake	
For making a light Pudding	109	To make a good Seed Cake	116
To make Almond Puddings		For making a cheap Seed Cake	
For making a cheap baked Rice Pudding		For making Mackeroons	
For making a Rice Pudding	110	To make Curd-cakes	117
For making a Batter Pudding		For making Cheesecakes	
For making a quaking Pudding		For making Rice Cheesecakes	118
To make a Pudding to bake		A good Cheese-cake	
For making a Potatoe Pudding		For making Lemon Cheese-cakes	
For making a Gooseberry Pudding	111	A proper Crust for Custards	119
For making excellent black Puddings		For making a Custard	
A good boiled Pudding		For making a Cream Custard	120
A good baked Pudding	112	To make a Gooseberry Custard	
A Plumb Pudding without Suet		For making common Buiscuits	
To make a boiled Pudding		To make a White-pot	121
To make white Puddings	113	For making plain Custards	
For making Marrow Puddings		For making an Almond Custard	
For making a Custard Pudding		For making a whip'd Sulibub	
Cakes, Cheesecakes, Custards.		How to make a Gooseberry Fool	122
How to make a Pound Cake	114	To make Apple-cream at any Time	
How to make a Plumb Cake		To make clouted Cream	
Shrewsberry Cakes	115	To make Quince Cream	123
To make a good Seed Cake		To make a Trifle Cream	
		To make Angellets	
		To make Bread without Yeast	124
		How to make a very good Tansie	

INDEX.

	Page		Page
To make Furmenty	125	preserve white or red Currant,	134
make a Sack Poffet		preserve Walnuts	
make gallendine Sauce for a Turkey	186	preserve Damsons, or black Plumbs	135
make Leach		preserve Currants	
To make Cheese Loaves		preserve Barberries	136
To make a fresh Cheese		preserve Rasberries	

Of Jellies.

		preserve Fruit green all the Year	
Currant Jelly	127	pickle Walnuts	
Calves Foot Jelly		preserve Walnuts whole	137
To make a chrystal Jelly	128	preserve Walnuts black	
Hartshorn Jelly		preserve green Plumbs	138
To make Jelly of Pippins or Codlins	129	put Plumbs in Jelly	

Of Candying.

		dry plumbs, pears, Apples, Grapes, &c.	139
To candy Cherries		preserve white ripe Grapes	
candy all Kind of Flowers, in Ways of Spanish Candy		preserve Gooseberries	
To candy all Kind of Fruitage, as Oranges, Lemon, Lettice-stocks, &c.	130	make Wafers	140
To candy Barberries and Grapes		make Conserve for Tarts all the Year	
candy Orange or Lemon Peels		keep Quinces all the Year	
candy Apricots			

Preserving and Confectionary.

Pickling and Preserving.

		To pickle Cucumbers	142
To preserve Cherries in Liquid	131	large Cucumbers in slices	
draw Jelly of Currants		small Cucumbers	143
preserve green Grapes	132	Oysters	
preserve Currants		Mellons or large Cucumbers	144
preserve Damsons		French Beans	145
preserve Grapes	133	Mushrooms	146
preserve Rasberries		Catchup of mushrooms	147
preserve Pippins		To pickle Lettice	

THE

	Page		Page
Walnuts		Birch Wine, as made	
Walnuts white	148	in Sussex	
small Onions		Sage Wine	157
red Cabbage		To make Elder Wine	
Cauliflowers	149	very excellent	
Asparagus to keep the whole Year		To make white Mead	159
		Raisin Wine	
Samphire	150	Black-cherry Wine	160
Beetroots and Turnips		Currant Wine	
		Damson Wine	161
Barberries		Rasberry Wine	
Grapes or Barberries		To fine wine the lisbon way	
Currants	151	clear Wine	162
preserve Cherries with the Leaves and Stalks green		recover Wine if turned sharp	
		make Cyder	163
pickle Gooseberries or Grapes		keep Gooseberries, Damsons, Bullace, Plumbs and Cherries in Bottles	
Currants for present Use			
Pidgeons	152	*Rulees for Marketing.*	
Tongues		For chusing Beef	164
Pork		For chusing Mutton	
Herrings or Mackerel	153	How to chuse Veal	165
Salmon		to chuse Lamb	
Lobsters	154	to chuse Pork	166
Tench		to chuse Venison	
Muscles or Cockles, Smelts to exceed Anchovies	155	Westphalia or English Hams	
		How to chuse Bacon	157
Purslain			
Verjuice		*Poultry.*	
To distill Verjuice for Pickles	156	to know a Capon	
		A Cock and Hen	
An excellent Way to make Vinegar, by which a Person lately acquired a good Fortune		Cock or Hen Turkey, or Turkey Poults	168
		A Goose	
		A Duck	
		Chickens	
Made Wines.		A Wild Duck	
Cowslip Wine	157	A Woodcock or Snipe	169
To make Mead		A Partridge	

INDEX.

	Page		Page
Pidgeons		to chuse Butter	
A Hare		to chuse Cheese	174
A Leverit	170	*Rules to be observed in dressing Provisions.*	
A Rabbit			

Chusing Fish.

	Page		Page
For chusing Place, Flounders and Dabs		Dishes that require a quarter of an Hour roasting	176
For chusing pickled Salmon	171	Joints that require half an Hour dressing	
fresh Salmon		Three quarters of an Hour	177
Whitings		An Hour and half	
pickled Sturgeon	172	Two Hours	
Cod		Three Hours	
Soals		*Names of the different Joints of Meat.*	
red Herrings			
Lyng			
Prawns and Shrimps		Beef	178
Crabs		Bacon. Mutton. Pork	179
Lobsters	173	Veal. Poultry. Herbs	180
Eggs		The London and Country Brewer	81
How to keep Eggs good			

POWELL's
COMPLETE
Book of *Cookery*,

Plain and easy Instructions for ROASTING *Butcher's Meat, &c.*

For Roasting in General.

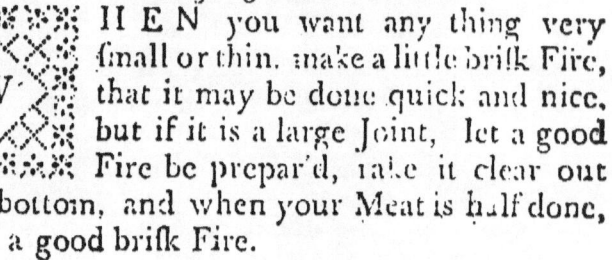

WHEN you want any thing very small or thin, make a little brisk Fire, that it may be done quick and nice, but if it is a large Joint, let a good Fire be prepar'd, rake it clear out at the bottom, and when your Meat is half done, stir up a good brisk Fire.

For Roasting Beef.

When you roast Beef, make up a strong lasting Fire, that it may penetrate into the heart of the Meat, else the inside will be raw when the outside is over done. When you think it is near enough, make your Fire burn brisker, in order to brown it. While it is roasting, baste it often with its own Dripping, and flour it well. The time for roasting is the same with that of boiling, a quarter of an Hour to every Pound of Meat.

If a Surloin or Rump, you must not salt it, but lay it a good Way from the Fire, baste it once or twice with Water and Salt, then with Butter; flour it, and keep basting with its own dripping. When the Smoak of it draws to the Fire it is near enough done.

If the Ribs, sprinkle them with a little Salt half an Hour before you lay it down; dry and flour it, then butter a piece of Paper very thick and fasten it on the Beef, put the buttered side next the Meat.

☞ Never salt your roast Beef before you lay it down to the Fire (except the Ribs) for that will draw out the Gravy.

When you keep it a few Days before you dress it, dry it well with a clean Cloth, and flour it all over, then hang it up where the Air may come to it.

For Roasting Mutton.

All Joints of Mutton, except a Leg, requires a brisker Fire then Beef. Baste it with Butter, and flour it often, but if it be very large, and you suspect it to be Ram Mutton, baste it well on first laying it down with Water and Salt, and that will take off the rankness. You must abate somewhat
of

of a quarter of an Hour of each Pound, especially when you roast a Shoulder or Neck.

☞ Always take off the Skin of a Breast of Mutton before you lay it down to the Fire.

To roast a Shoulder of Mutton with Thyme.

Draw your Shoulder of Mutton, and when it is half roasted save the Gravy, and cut a good deal of the inside off it, and mince it gross, and boil it in a Dish with the Gravy and Thyme, Claret Wine and sliced Nutmeg, and when your Shoulder is roasted, lay it in the Dish with sliced Lemon, but remember to scotch your Mutton in roasting, as you do in boiling.

For roasting a Leg of Mutton with Cockles.

Stuff it all over with Cockles, then roast it; garnish it with Horse-raddish.

To roast a Leg or Shoulder of Mutton with Oysters.

When you open the Oysters, save the liquor, then season them with Pepper, and a little Cloves and Mace, and Herbs finely chopped, and the yolks of 2 or 3 Eggs chopped small and some Currants parboiled a little, then stuff your Shoulder of Mutton thick with your Oysters, then season it and lay it to the Fire and roast it, then take the rest of your Oysters, and boil them with a little Whitewine, and some Butter, this is sauce for your Shoulder of Mutton, when your Oysters are opened you may parboil them in their own liquor, then take them out and season them—Or take a Leg that has been two or three Days butchered. Stuff it all over with Oysters, then roast it, and garnish with Horse-raddish.

To roll a Breast of Mutton.

First bone the Mutton, then make a favory forced meat for it, and wash it with the batter of Eggs then spread the forced meat on it; roll it in a collar and bind it with Pack-thread, then roast it, put under it a Regalia of Cucumbers.

To roast a Chine of Mutton.

First raise up the skin from the Chine-bone, a little downwards; then take some slices of lean Bacon seasoned with Pepper, and roll'd Cives and shred Parsley, and spread them over the Chine, and lay lards of Bacon over them, and turn the skin over it; tie the Chine with Tape and put white Paper over to prevent discolouring it, roast it at a clear Fire; in roasting throw Crumbs of white Bread over it: when enough, serve it with a Regalia of Cucumbers.

For roasting Mutton, Venison Fashion.

Get a fat Hind-quarter of Mutton and cut the Leg like a Haunch of Venison, then rub it well with Salt-petre, and hang it in a moist place for two Days, wiping it two or three times a Day with a clean Cloth, then put it into a pan, and having boiled a quarter of an Ounce All-spice in a quart of red Wine, pour it boiling hot over your Mutton, and cover it close for two Hours, then take it out, spit it, lay it to the Fire and constantly baste it with the same liquor and Butter. If you have a good quick Fire, and your Mutton not very large, it will be ready in a Hour and a half, then take it up and send it to Table with some Gravy in one Cup, and sweet sauce in another.

For roasting Veal.

If the Fillet, ſtuff it with Parſley, Marjoram and Thyme, a ſprig of Savory, a ſmall Onion, a bit of Lemon-peel, cut very ſmall, Pepper, Salt, Mace, Nutmeg, Crumbs of Bread, four Eggs and a quarter of a Pound of Butter or Marrow mixed with a little Flour to make it ſtiff, put half of it into the Udder, and the other half into the holes made in the fleſhy Part.

If a Shoulder, make the ſame ſort of Stuffing and baſte it with Milk till half done, then flour it and baſte it with Butter.

If a Breaſt, roaſt it with the Caul on 'till it is enough, and Skewer the Sweet-bread on the backſide the Breaſt; and when it is near done, take off the Caul, baſte it and dredge it with a little Four. All theſe are to be ſent to Table with melted Butter, and garniſh with ſliced Lemon.

If a Fillet or Loin not ſtuffed, take care to paper the Fat, that as little as poſſible may be loſt. All Joints are to be laid at a diſtance from the Fire, till ſoaked, then nearer the Fire. When you lay it down baſte it with good Butter (except it be the Shoulder, and that may be done the ſame, if you like it better) and when it is near enough, baſte it again, and dredge it with a little Flour.

An admirable way to roaſt a Calves Head.

Take a Calves Head and boil it an Hour and a half; when cold, lard it with Lemon-peel and then ſpit it: when enough, make good ſavoury Sauce, as you do for a haſh'd Head, and put into it forc'd Meat-balls, fryed Sweet-breads, Eggs and Clary,

Clary, a little Bacon, some Truffels and Morels, Mushrooms and Oysters, and a little Lemon-juice and mix it all well together with the sauce and pour it over the Head.

Lamb or Veal.

All young Meats ought to be thoroughly done, therefore do not take Lamb or Veal off the spit till you see they drop a white Gravy.

For roasting Calves Liver.

Lard it well with large slices of Bacon, fasten it on the spit, roast at a gentle Fire, and serve it up with good Veal Gravy or melted Butter.

For roasting a Pig.

Take Sage shred very small, grated Bread, Salt, a little Pepper, and the Yolks of four Eggs, mix them well with a little white Wine till they come to a Consistency; then put them into the belly of the Pig, sew it up, and after having rubbed the skin over with Butter, put it on the spit: Keeping it continually basting and wipeing with a clean Cloth and turning very fast till it is enough. One Hour will roast a midling Pig, if large more time must be allowed. When enough take the Pudding out of the belly, mix it with Gravy and the brains of the Pig: Sweet sauce is to be made the same Way, only add a few Currants, some Sugar, Nutmeg, and a little white Wine.

Another Way.

Take and wipe it quite dry with a clean Cloth, then take some Crumbs of Bread, a piece of Butter, of each a quarter of a Pound, Parsley, Thyme, Sage, Sweet-majoram, Salt, Pepper and Nutmeg,

with

with the Yolks of two Eggs; mix them together, and sew it up in the belly, and then spit it; flour it very thick and lay it to the Fire, taking Care that your Fire burns well at both Ends, or hang a a flat Iron in the middle of the Grate till it does; continue flouring it till you find the Crackling hard then wipe it clean with a Cloth wetted in salt and water, and baste it with Butter. When the Gravy begins to run put your basons in the dripping pan to receive it. When you find it is enough take about a quarter of a Pound of Butter, put it in a coarse clean Cloth, and having made a clear brisk Fire, rub the Pig all over with it till the Crackling is quite crisp and then take it from the Fire. Cut off the Head, and cut the Pig in two down the back, then take out the spit; having cut the Ears off, place one at each End, and also cut the Head in two and place one at each side, and serve it up with some good Beef Gravy, mix the Gravy from the Pig, and the Brains bruised, and a little dried Sage shred small; pour all these together into the Dish and serve it up.

For roasting Pork.

Pork should lie twelve Hours at least in Salt, before you put it down to roast, then flour it well but very little basting will serve, except you roast it without cutting the skin, and then you must keep it basting and turning very fast, as you would do a Pig, to preserve it from blistering, or parting from the flesh. This is a very luscious Meat, and requires the same time as Beef and a strong Fire, for it will be pernicious if eaten with Gravy in it that

has

has the leaſt Tincture of redneſs, is very apt to ſurfeit. The common as well as the moſt wholſome ſauce is Apple-ſauce and Muſtard—The beſt way of roaſting the Leg is to parboil, then take off the ſkin and lay it down, baſte it with Butter, then take a little Pepper and Salt, a little Sage ſhred fine, a few Crumbs of Bread and a little Nutmeg; throw theſe all over it all the time it is roaſting, then put a little drawn Gravy into the Diſh with the Crumbs that drop from it.——Some like the Knuckle ſtuffed with Sage and Onion ſhred ſmall with a little Pepper and Salt, Gravy and Apple ſauce to it; this they call a mock Gooſe. The Spring or Hand of Pork if very young and roaſted like Pig eats very well, otherwiſe it is beſt boiled. The beſt Way to dreſs Pork Griſkins is to roaſt them, baſte them with Butter and Crumbs of Bread, Sage, and a little Pepper and Salt: but ſome like them better broiled. The Spa-rib ſhould be baſted with a bit of Butter, a very little flour, and ſome Sage ſhred ſmall, and ſerved up with Apple-ſauce.

When you roaſt a Loin, take a ſharp Penknife and cut the ſkin acroſs to make the Crackling eat the better, The Chine you need not cut at all.

Obſerve

Observe in Roasting POULTRY,

THAT if your Fire is not very brisk and clear, when you lay your Poultry down to roast, it will not eat near so sweet, or look so beautiful to the Eye.

For roasting a *Capon*.

Half an Hour will roast the largest Capon, provided your fire is strong and brisk, keep it well basted. The best Sauce is a rich Gravy, well relish'd with Spice and Ricamboll or Shallot.

Pullets with Eggs or without.

A Pullet with Eggs will take somewhat more roasting than a Capon: Egg sauce is more proper and most commonly eaten with it. If she be without Egg, she will take less time in roasting than a Capon. Gravy sauce is also best with this.

Chickens.

A quarter of an Hour will roast a well-grown Chicken, the sauce is Parsley and Butter, or Gravy.

Tame *Duck.*

Shred some Sage and Onion very small, mix it with Pepper and Salt, and put into the Belly of the Duck: When it is enough done take out the Stuffing, and mingle it with a good deal of red Wine and Gravy for sauce.

For roasting a *Turkey*.

Take half a pound of Suet, a little Parsley, Sweet Marjoram, Thyme, a sprig of Winter Savory,

vory, a bit of Lemon-peal, half a Nutmeg grated a little Mace, Salt, cut your Herbs very small, chop them as small as possible and mix all together with three Eggs, and as much grated Bread as will make it of a proper consistence; then fill the Crop of your Turkey with it, paper the Breast and lay it down at a good distance from the Fire, When the smoak begins to draw to the Fire, and it looks plump baste it again, and dredge it again with a little flower, soon after take it up and send it to the Table with some strong Beef Gravy; garnish the Dish with Lemon.

A Turkey must be well flower'd and basted, and roasted with a strong fire, especially if the Belly be stuffed with Oysters, which you must take out as soon as it comes off the Spit, and put them into melted Butter with Gravy, if no Oysters, less Time will roast it, and put no Butter to your Gravy.—Or, you may make the following sauce; take a little white Gravy. Catchup, a few Bread crumbs and a little whole Pepper, let them boil well together: put to them a little flower, and a lump of Butter, which pour upon the Turkey. You may lay round your Turkey, forced Meat Balls. garnish your Dish as before.

For roasting a Goose.

Chop Onion and Sage small mixed with some Pepper and Salt, and a bit of Butter, and put them into the Goose's belly, then spit it, singe it with white Paper, dredge it with a little Flower and baste it with its own Dripping. When it is enough (which is known by the Legs being Tender) take

it

it up and pour into it some good Beef Gravy, the sauce in the Dish must also be the same, and serve it up in the same Dish, and set Mustard and Sugar for those who like it, and Apple-sauce in a Bason.

How to truss a *Goose*.

Let only the thick joints of the Legs and Wings be left to the Body, the Pinions and Feet should be cut of and go with the other Giblets, which consist of the Gizzard and Liver, and the Head and Neck. Cut a hole at the bottom of the Apron of the Goose and draw the Rump thro' it; then put a skewer through the small part of the Leg, and thro' the Body near the Back, and another through the thiner part of the Wing, and thro' the Body near the back and then you have done.

For roasting a *Woodcock*.

Truss your Woodcock, and draw it under the Leg, take out the bitter part, and put in the Guts again. Whilst the Woodcock is roasting, baste it with Butter, set under it an earthen Dish with a slice of toasted Bread in it, and let the Woodcock drop upon it: Your Woodcock will take about half an Hour in Roasting if you have a brisk Fire. When you dish it up, lay the Toast under it, and serve it up with sauce made of Gravy and Butter, a little Lemon and a spoonful or two of red Wine, and pour a little over the Toast.

Another way for roasting *Larks*.

Let them be trussed handsomely on the Back, but neither draw them nor cut off their Feet. Laid them with small Lardons, or else spit them on a wooden skewer with a small bit of Bacon between them;

them; when they are near roasted enough, dredge them with fine Salt and fine crumbs of Bread. When they are ready, rub the Dish you intend to serve them in with a Shalot, and serve them with a sauce made of Claret, the Juice of two or three Oranges and a little shred Ginger, set it over the Fire a little while and beat them up with a piece of Butter.

You may use the same Sauce with broiled Larks, which you must open on the Breast when you lay them on the Gridiron.

To roast a *Wild Duck*.

Wild Duck or any other Wild Fowl should be roasted with the Spit made hot before you lay them on; otherwise the inside will be raw and the outside too much done: They must all in general be constantly basted with Butter, and their own driping. The Sauce for a tame Duck serves for all kind of Wild Fowl; except a Patridge which shou'd be basted with Butter, and strewed with grated Bread; and the Sauce made of grated bread Yolk of Eggs, white Wine and Gravy well spiced.

How to truss *Easterlings, Ducks, Teals* and *Widgeons*.

When you draw it lay aside the Gizard and Liver, and take out the Neck, taking care to leave the Skin of the Neck full enough to cover that part where the Neck was cut off. Next cut off the Pinions, and raize up the whole Legs 'till they are in the middle, and press them between the Body of the Fowl and the stump of the Wings, then twist the Feet and set the bottom of them
towards

towards the Body of the Fowl, and put a skewer through the Fowl, between the lower joint next the Thigh and the Foot, taking hold of the ends of the stump of the Wings, then the Legs will stand upright.

A good *Sauce* for *Teal, Mallard, Ducks*, &c.

Take a quantity of Veal Gravy according to the bigness of the Dish or wild Fowl, seasoned with Pepper and Salt, squeeze in the Juice of two Oranges and a little Claret. This will serve all sorts of wild Fowl.

For roasting a *Hare*.

A Hare is best when Larded; but if this is not thought proper, you may make a Pudding of grated Bread, the Liver of the Hare minced small, Parsley, Thyme, Winter Savory, Sweet Marjarom, Salt, Pepper a few Cloves beaten, the Yolks of three Eggs wetted with Claret, and put into the Belly, which when sewed up put it on the Spit, baste it with Cream 'till half done, then with its own Dripping; but keep it always moist. Mix half a Pint of Claret with very strong and high-season'd Gravy sauce, an Hour will roast it.

For roasting a *Hare* another way.

Lard it, Spit it, and while it is roasting baste it with Milk or Cream, then serve it with thick Claret sauce.

Another Way.

Take the Liver of a Hare, grated Bread, some fat bacon, a Shalot, an Anchovy, a little Winter savoury and a little Nutmeg, beat all these into a Paste and put them into the Belly of the Hare, baste the Hare with ſtale Beer, put a little bit of Bacon in the Pan, when it is half roaſted baſte it with Butter. For ſauce take melted butter and a bit of Winter Savory.

Another Way.

Make a Pudding of grated Bread and the Heart and Liver par boiled and chopped ſmall, with beef ſuet and ſweet Herbs mix'd with Marrow, Cream Spice and Egg,, then ſew the Belly and roaſt it. When it is roaſted let your Herbs be ſerved up with Cream Gravy, or Claret.

How to truſs a *Hare*.

In caſing a Hare, when you come to the Ears put a ſkewer juſt between the Head and the Skin, and raize it up by degrees 'till both the Ears are ſtriped, and take of the reſt as uſual. Then twiſt the Head over the Back, and put two ſkewers in the Ears to make them ſtand almoſt upright, and to keep the Head in a proper poſition, then puſh up the joints of the Shoulder blade towards the Back, and put a ſkewer betwen the joint thro' the bottom jow to keep it ſteady. and another ſkewer through the lower branch of the Leg and thro' the Ribs to keep the blade-bone up-right and another thro' the point of the ſame branch, then bend both Legs in between the Haunches ſo as to make their points meet under the ſcut, and take care to ſkewer them faſt with two ſkewers.—It's common to ſend them to a Poulterer to be truſſed.

☞ A Hare may alſo be truſſed ſhort, in the manner of a Rabbit for boiling.

For roasting *Rabbits*.

Put them down to a moderate Fire and baste them with butter, then dredge them with flour, and melt some good butter, and having boiled the Livers with a bunch of Parsley, chop them small, put half into the Butter and pour it into the dish, and garnish it with the other half.

French Sauce for *Rabbits*.

Onions minced small, fried and mingled with Mustard and Pepper.

Another Way.

Or baste your Rabbits well with butter, keep them forty Minutes at the Fire, which should be brisk but not too strong: For sauce mince the Liver small and put no butter to it.

How to truss a *Rabbit* for roasting.

Case the whole Rabbit except the lower joints of the fore Legs and those you should chop off; then put a skewer through the middle of the Haunches, after you have laid them flat, and the fore legs which are called the Wings, must be turned so that the small Joints may be pushed into the body through the ribs. This is a single Rabbit, and has the spit put thro' the head and body, but the skewer take hold of the spit to preserve the Haunches. But if you truss a couple of Rabbits there should be seven skewers, and then the spit passed through between the skewers without touching the Rabbets.

Note. You may truss it short in the same manner as for boiling and roast it.

For roasting a Haunch of *Venison*.

First spit it, then take a little Wheat flour and Water, knead and roll it very thin, tie it over the fat part of the Venison with Packthread; if it be a large Haunch it will take four Hours roasting, and a middle Haunch three Hours, keep basting all the Time you roast it, when you dish it up put a little Gravy in the dish, and sweet sauce in a bason. Half an Hour before you draw your Venison take of the Paste and baste it, and let it be a light brown.

Another Way.

After the Haunch is spitted, beat the Whites of three or four Eggs and sprinkle in some of the best flour, and rub it over your Meat with a Feather, baste it with sweet butter and dredge it with flour. For your sauce boil Claret, a little Pepper, Mace, Salt, Gravy and butter; thicken it with grated bread.

To roast *Tripe*.

Take the best Roll of Tripe you can get, and put it into Water and Salt for twelve Hours, then take it out and dry it well, and cut it in half. For your seasoning take Suet, Thyme, Parsley, and bread crumbled fine, of each an equal quantity; a little Lemon-peal, Pepper, Salt and Nutmeg: Mix these well all together with the Yolk of an Egg then take half your Tripe and spread the above Ingredients upon it on the fat side, then put the other half upon it, and roll it as hard as you can, and bind it with a fillet, then put the spit thro' it and baste it with Butter; it will take as much
roasting

roasting as a fillet of Veal. The sauce is only butter and Gravy: When it is done take off the fillet, and serve it up.

To roast a Tongue and Udder.

Boil the Tongue a little, blanch it and lard it with Bacon, the length of an Inch, being first seasoned with Nutmeg, Pepper and Cinnamon, and stuff the Udder full of Cloves: Then spit and roast them, baste them with sweet Butter and serve them up with Claret sauce, garnish with sliced Lemon.

Another Way.

Parboil your Tongue or Udder, then stick ten or twelve Cloves in it. and when it is ready take it up and send it to Table with some Gravy and sweet sauce.

Roasting a Pickled Neat's Tongue.

First soak it, then boil it 'till the skin will peel off and then skin it, and stick it with Cloves, about two Inches asunder, then put it on a spit, and wrap a Veal Caul over it and roast it till enough; then take off the Caul and just froth it up and serve it in a Dish with Gravy, and some Vennison or Claret sauce in a Plate; garnish it with Raspings of Bread sifted and Lemon sliced.

To roast Lobsters.

Take a Lobster or as many as you will when alive and bind them to a spit with Pack-thread, with the Claws out strait, and the same time will be required for roasting as boiling, and baste them with Vinegar and Butter, and if you please you may tie a bunch of Herbs to a Stick and dip in Butter and Vinegar and baste with that, and mind in the roasting to salt them, serve them up as they come off the spit, with Butter in a China Cup.

To roast a Pike.

Spit your Pike at length with a splinter on each side, with a bunch of sweet herbs and an Onion stuck full of Cloves, and three Bay-leaves in the Belly, and wound about with thread to fasten it; then take a large bunch of sweet Herbs and put Butter on them, and baste with it instead of a basting Ladle, and so roast it: For the sauce have three Onions stuck with Cloves boiled in white Wine, Anchovies, Bay-leaves and Butter thicken'd with grated Bread.

Plain and easy Instructions for Boiling Meat, &c.

YOU must put all fresh Meat into the Water boiling hot, and your salt Meat when the Water is quite cold, unless you apprehend it is not salted quite enough, for the putting into hot Water strikes in the Salt.

Lamb, Veal, and Chickens, boil much whiter in a Linen Cloth, with a little Milk in the Water.

Observe that the Time sufficient for dressing different Joints depends on their size. A Leg of Mutton of about seven or eight Pounds will take two Hours boiling. A young Fowl about half an Hour. A middle-sized Leg of Lam about an Hour

Hour and a quarter. A thick piece of Beef of twelve or fourteen Pounds, will take about two Hours and a half after the Water boils, if you put in the Beef when your Water is cold; and so in Proportion to the thickness and weight of the Piece; but all Kind of Victuals take somewhat more time in frosty Weather; upon the whole, the best Rule to be observed is to allow a quarter of an Hour to every Pound. when the Joint is put into boiling Water.

In boiling Beef.

Let your pot be large enough to contain a sufficient quantity of Water for it to have room to wabble about, and be sure before you put it on, to make a good strong Fire, so that it may never cease boiling from the minute it begins, till it is thoroughly done. As for the Time of boiling you may allow a quarter of an Hour to every Pound of Beef except Brisket, which requires more by reason of its being so very fibrous.

To boil Mutton.

Mutton takes not up altogether so much Time or Water as Beef, yet it must not be cramped in too small a Pot, for if it is it will be tough, and the colour spoiled. If you make Broth put in no more Water then will just cover it, and after you have taken the Scum off which must be raised by throwing in some Salt, and put in what thickening the Family likes, whether Rice, Barley or Oatmeal, let it be close stopped till enough.

To boil a Leg of Mutton with Stuffing.

Take a Leg of Mutton and stuff it, for the stuffing take some Beef-suet, and some sweet Herbs, chop them small, and stuff it, then boil it, and put in a handful of sweet Herbs, cut them small mingle a hard Egg among the Herbs, and strew it upon the Mutton, melt some Butter and Vinegar put it into a Dish and send it in.

To boil Veal.

A great inducement to eating heartily of boiled Veal is the whiteness of it: You should therefore not only be particular careful in taking off the Scum, but also tie the Meat in a Cloth, and the Skin will then look of a delicate clearness. — The same care ought to be taken of Lamb, especially *House*; for it being of a more delicate Texture than the Grass, is more liable to imbibe any disagreeable Tincture. Both ought to be well boiled, as indeed should all young Meat, or it is unwholsome,

For boiling a Leg of Lamb, with the Loin fryed about it.

Boil the Lamb, then lay it in the Dish and pour a little Parsley and Butter over it; and lay your fried Lamb round it, cut some Asparagus the size of Pease, boil them green, and lay them round your your Lamb in spoonfuls, and garnish the Dish with crisp'd Parsley.

A Leg of Lamb boiled with Chickens round it.

When your Lamb is boiled pour over it Parsley and Butter; lay your Chickens round your Lamb and

and pour over your Chickens a little white fricaſſee Sauce. Garniſh your Diſh with Sippets and Lemons.

To boil Pickled Pork.

Firſt waſh your Pork, then ſcrape it clean; and put it into the Pot when the Water is cold, and boil it till the Rind is tender.

Pork requires much boiling and ſhould never be dreſſed without Salting, for there is a juice between the Rind and the Fat, which if not well purged out, breeds bad Humours.

For keeping Meat hot.

Set a Diſh over a pan of boiling Water, cover the Diſh with a deep cover ſo as not to touch the Meat, and lay a Cloth over all. This way will keep your Meat hot a long Time, and it is better then over roaſting and ſpoiling the Meat. The Steam of the Water keeps the Meat hot, and does not draw the Gravy out, or dry it up; whereas if you ſet a Diſh of Meat any Time over a chaffing Diſh of Coals it will dry up all the Gravy and ſpoil the Meat.

To boil Greens.

When you boil Greens, firſt ſoak them two Hours in Water and Salt, or elſe boil them in Water and Salt in a Copper by themſelves, with a great quantity of Water.

Uſe no iron Pans, &c. for they are not proper, but let them be Copper, Braſs, or Silver.

For boiling Sprouts and Cabbage.

All ſorts of Sprouts and Cabbage muſt be boiled in a great deal of Water. Always throw Salt in to your Water before you put your Greens in. When the ſtalks are tender, or fall to the bottom they are enough, then take them off; before they looſe their Colour.

To dreſs Spinage.

Take care to pick and waſh it very clean; put it in a ſauce-pan that will juſt hold it, throw a little Salt over it and cover the Pan cloſe. Don't put any Water in, but ſhake the Pan often: as ſoon as you find them covered with their own Liquor and are tender, they are done; then ſqeeze them well between two clean Plates, and ſerve them up with Butter in a Baſon.

For boiling Carrots.

Scrape them very clean, and when they are enough rub them in a clean Cloth, and ſlice them into a Plate and pour ſome melted Butter over them If they are young ſpring Carrots, half an Hour will boil them; if large an Hour, but old Sandwich Carrots will take two Hours.

For boiling Caulliflowers.

Take off all the green Part and cut the Flowers into four quarters, and lay them into Water for an Hour then put the Caulliflowers into ſome boiling Milk and Water, and be ſure to ſkim the ſaucepan well. When the ſtalks are tender take them carefully up, and put them into a Cullinder to drain, then diſh them and ſerve them with Butter in a Cup.

For boiling Brocolie.

Strip off all the little branches, till you come to the top one, then take a Knife and peel off all the
hard

hard outside skin, which is on the stalks and little branches, wash them put them in a Stew-pan of Water and some Salt. in it when it boils and the Stalks are tender it is enough, then send it to table with Butter in a Cup.

The French eat Oil and Vinegar with it.

For boiling French Beans.

String them, then cut them in two, and afterwards across. Lay them into Water and Salt and when the Pan boils put in some Salt and the Beans, when they are tender they are enough, they will be soon done. Take care they don't loose their fine green. Lay them in a Plate and serve them with Butter in a Cup.

For boiling Asparagus.

Scrape all the Stalks very carefully till they look white, then cut them all even alike and tie them in little bundles, then throw them into a Stew-pan of boiling Water, put in some Salt, and let the Water keep boiling; and when they are tender take them up, then make a Toast and dip it in the Asparagus Liquor and lay it in the Dish: Pour a little Butter over the Toast, then lay the Asparagus on the Toast all round the Dish with the white bottoms outward. Put your Butter in a Bason and send it to Table.

For boiling Artichokes.

Wring off the Stalks, and put them into the Water cold with the tops downwards, that all the Sand may boil out. When the Water boils, an Hour and a quarter will do them.

For

For boiling POULTRY.

To boil Pullets and Oysters.

BOIL them in Water and Salt with a piece of Bacon: For sauce melt a Pound of Butter, with a little white Wine and strong Broth, and a Quart of Oysters, then put your pullets in a Dish, cut the Bacon and lay about them, with a Pound or two of fry'd Sausages, and garnish it with sliced Lemon.

To boil Fowls.

Boil them as aforesaid: For the sauce toss up Sweet-breads, Artichoke-bottoms, Lamb-stones, Cocks-combs, and hard Eggs, all sliced in strong Broth and white Wine, with Asparagus-tops and Spice; thicken it with a bit of Butter kneaded in Flour, garnish the Dish with sliced Lemon.

To dress Chickens and Asparagus.

First force your Chickens with good Forc'd-meat, and boil them white, cut your Asparagus-tops about an Inch in length, and parboil it in Water, a little Flour and Butter, and drain it well then put in your Sauce-pan a little Butter and Salt and dissolve it gently, add to the Asparagus minc'd Parsley and sweet Cream, some Fennel and Nutmeg grated, Pepper and Salt, then stew it over a gentle Charcoal Fire, squeezing in it some Lemon-juice, and so serve it on your Chickens.

For boiling Chickens.

Take four or five Chickens, as you would have your

your Dish in bigness; if they be small ones scald them, then pluck them which will make them whiter, then draw them and take out the breast-bone; wash them, truss them, cut off the Heads and Necks, tie them up in a Napkin, and boil them in Milk and and Water, and some Salt, about five and twenty Minutes will do them. They are best for being killed the over Night before you use them.

For making Sauce to the Chickens

Boil the Necks, Livers and Gizards in Water, and when they are enough, strain off the Gravy, and put a spoonfull of Oyster-pickle to them, break the Livers small, mix some Gravy, and rub them through a Hair-sieve with the back of a Spoon; then put a Spoonful of Cream to it, some Lemon, and Lemon-peel grated; thicken it with some Butter and Flour. Let your sauce be no thicker than Cream, poor it upon your Chickens. Garnish your Dish with Sipets and Mushrooms, and slices of Lemon.

To boil a Turkey with Oysters.

Take half a Pint of Water, half an Anchovy, three Spoonfulls of Oyster Liquor, thicken it well with Flour over the Fire; then stew your Oysters with the rest of the Liquor, and two blades of Mace, some whole Pepper, then take out your Oysters and strain all the Liquor: when your Turkey is almost ready put all your Sauce together with a piece of Butter, and a Spoonful or two of Gravy, a Spoonful of white Wine, some Lemon-juice,

juice, and shake it over the Fire, and pour it over the Turkey and serve it up.

For boiling a Turkey.

Draw and truss your Turkey, cut off the Feet, and cut down the Breast-bone with a Knife, then sow up the skin again, stuff the Breast with the following Stuffing.

For making Stuffing to a boiled Turkey.

Boil a Sweet-bread of Veal, chop it fine with some Lemon-peel, a Handful of Bread Crumbs, some Beef-suet, part of the Liver, a Spoonful or two of Cream, with Pepper, Salt, Nutmeg, and two Eggs, mix all together and stuff your Turkey with part of the Stuffing, the rest may be boiled or fried to lay round it, dredge it with some Flour tie it up in a Cloth, and boil it with Milk and Water; if the Turkey is young an Hour and a Quarter will do it.

For making Sauce to a boiled Turkey.

Take a pint of Oysters, two Spoonfuls of Cream Juice of a Lemon, a little small white Gravy, and Salt to your Taste, thicken it with Flour and Butter, then pour it over the Turkey and serve it up lay round the Turkey fried Oysters, and the forced meat. Garnish the Dish with Mushrooms, Oysters and slices of Lemon.

To boil Pigeons.

When you have well cleansed and trussed your Pigeons, stuff their bellies with Parsley, and be sure to take off the Scum as often as it rises. Something more than a quarter of an Hour boils them. Whatever you boil, either of Flesh or Fowl, should

should be set over a brisk Fire, that it may be kept constantly in Motion; for if it ceases, though never so small a Time, the Gravy drains out into the Water.

To boil Pigeons.

Stuff your Pigeons with sweet Herbs, chop'd Bacon a little grated Bread, a little Butter, Spice, and the Yolk of an Egg, then boil them in strong Broth, white Wine Vinegar, Mace, Salt, Nutmeg and Parsley minc'd, and drawn Butter, garnish your Dish with sliced Lemon and Barberries.

To boil Ducks.

When they be half boiled take a quart of the Liquor and strain it, and put a quart of white Wine and some whole Mace, Cloves and Nutmegs sliced Cinnamon, and a few Onions shred a bundle of sweet Herbs, a few Capers, and some Camphire, when it is boiled put some Sugar to season it to your palate.

For boiling a Goose.

Season your Goose, with Pepper and Salt for four or five Days, then boil it about an Hour; and serve it hot with Cabbage, Carrots, Turnips, or Cauliflowers, tossed up with Butter.

To boil Geese.

Let them be powdered, and then fill their bellies with Oatmeal, which should first be steep'd in Milk or a little small Broth, warm: You may season it as you please with Herbs Spice and Onions; some will put in Beef-suet, but that is as you like. When you have filled the Belly, tie it at the

Neck and Vent, boil it with Greens and Roots, and serve it up.

For boiling Rabbets.

Truſs them for boiling, and lard them with Bacon; then boil them quick and white. For ſauce take the boiled Liver and ſhred it with fat Bacon, toſs theſe up together in ſome good Gravy, white Wine Vinegar, Nutmeg, Mace and Salt, ſet Parſley, minced Barberries, and drawn Butter. Lay your Rabbits in a Diſh, and pour the ſauce all over them. Garniſh it with ſliced Lemon and Barberries.

Boiling Rabits with Sauſages.

Take a couple of Rabbits, and when almoſt boiled, put in a pound of Sauſages, and boil with them, when done enough, diſh the Rabbits, placing the Sauſages round the Diſh, with ſome fried ſlices of Bacon. For ſauce put Muſtard and melted Butter beat up together in a Cup and ſerve them hot.

For boiling a Ham.

Lay one of about ſixteen Pounds into cold Water two Hours, then waſh it clean, and boil it very ſlow the firſt Hour, and very briſk an Hour and a half more. Then take off the Rind, and ſprinkle it over with ſome raſping of Bread, but ſome who are very curious will wrap it up in Hay, before they put it into the Copper, in order to make it look red.

To boil a Tongue.

Lay a dried Tongue in warm Water for ſix Hours, then lay it three Hours in cold Water. Then

Then take it out and boil it three Hours which will be sufficient. If your Tongue be just out of Pickle it must lay three Hours in cold Water, and then boil it till it will peel.

Another Way.

A Tongue if Salt, put in the Pot over Night and do not let it boil till about three Hours before Dinner, and then boil it all that three Hours; if fresh out of the Pickle two Hours, and put it in when the Water boils.

BOILING FISH.

To boil a Salmon.

WASH it and let it bleed well in the Water, then let it drain, after which put it into boiling Water, take out the Liver when about three Parts done, and braid it with Ketchup, which mingled with the Butter will make exceeding rich sauce. This sort of Dish takes almost as much boiling as Mutton.

To boil Pike.

Wash your Pike clean, then truss it round with the Tail in its Mouth, and its Back scotched in three places; then throw it in the boiling Water with a good deal of Salt and Vinegar, three or four blades of Mace, and the peal of a whole Lemon: Let it boil fast at first, for that will make the Pike eat firm, but more slow afterwards. The Time must be proportioned to the bigness of the Fish, but

but half an Hour is enough for a very large one. The best sauce for this is plain Butter with a few Shrimps and a Seville Orange.

To boil fresh Cod:

Mix a great deal of the best white Wine Vinegar with the Water in which you boil fresh Cod, Lemon peel, Salt, Mace and Cloves, otherwise the Fish will taste waterish, be very flabby, and liable to break in the Kettle. The sauce for this cannot be too rich, and if you are allowed it, spare neither Ketchup, Body of a Lobster, or Crab, Oysters and Shrimps, but if you have not all these at hand, put in as many of them as you can. You mak know when it is enough, as you may all Fish, by the drooping out of the Eyes.

To boil Barrel Cod, or any other Salt Fish.

All Kinds of Salt Fish must lie in the Water proportionable to its Saltness: Trust not therefore to those you buy it of, but taste a bit of one of the Flanks. The sauce for it is Butter, Eggs, Mustard and Parsnips, or Potatoes.

To boil a Cod's Head.

Set your Kettle on the Fire with Water, Vinegar and Salt, a Faggot of sweet Herbs, and a large Onion; when the liquor boils, put in the Head, on a Fish-plate; in the boiling put in cold Water and Vinegar, when it's boiled drain it well, and for sauce take Gravy and Claret, boiled up with a Faggot of sweet Herbs and an Onion, two or three Anchovies, half a Pint of Shrimps, and the Meat of a Lobster shred fine, then put the Head on a Dish, pour the sauce thereon, stick small Toasts on

the

the Head, and lay about it the Spawn, Melt and Liver. Garnish it with Parsley, boiled Barberries, and Lemon.

To boil a Jowl of Salmon.

Take a faggot of sweet Herbs, a little Lemon-peel, some Mace, Pepper, Salt and Nutmeg, two Quarts of Water, a pint of Vinegar, an Onion stuck with Cloves, and set these over the Fire to boil a good while, then put in your Fish, half a quarter of an Hour boils it: take it up and drain it: For sauce take strong Broth and two Anchovies boiled and strained, half a pint of Claret, a little Lemon-juice, a Pound of Butter, a little Flour, with some shrimps tofs'd up therein, pour this on the Fish. Garnish with Lemon peel.

To make an excellent Sauce for Salmon.

Put into the Liquor of the Salmon, when you boil it, Salt, Vinegar and Mace; take a quarter of a Pint of the Liquor and draw your Butter with it, mince into it, an Anchovy wash'd clean, some Lemon-juice and Nutmeg, half a pint of Shrimps, two Spoonfuls of white Wine; with Ketchup and Mushrooms.

To boil a Turburt or Poliburt.

Your Fish being made clean, make a Bouillion of half Wine and Water, and season it with Spice, Salt, Herbs and Lemon-peel; let it boil some time before you put in your Fish, and boil it half an Hour, scum it as it boils, then take it up and drain it, you may serve it on a clean Napkin with Fish-sauce upon sipets or plain Butter.

For

For BROILING.

WHEN you broil any thing, let it be over a Stove of Charcoal, rather then Seacoal; turn your Meat very often. Whatever you broil or roast, do not Salt till it is put to the Fire; if you do, the Gravy will entirely run out, and the Meat become hard.

To broil Chickens.

Take fat Chickens, and slit them down the back; season them with Pepper and Salt, and lay them on a clear Fire, not too fierce; lay the inside next the Fire, when half done, turn them very often and baste them well, and strew on the raspings of French Bread sifted fine. For sauce, take a handful of Sorrel; dip it in hot Water, then drain it; add half a pint of Gravy, a Shallot shred small, a little Parsley and Thyme, a bit of Butter to thicken it, lay the Sorrel in heaps, and pour on the sauce.

Another Way.

First slit them down the back, then season them with Pepper and Salt, and lay them on a clear fire at a good distance, let the inside lay next the fire till it is above half done, then turn them, and take care the fleshy side do not burn, and let them be of a fine brown, your sauce may be good Gravy with Mushrooms; and garnish with Lemon and the Livers broiled, the Gizards cut, slashed, and broiled with Pepper and Salt.

To broil *Sheep* or *Hog's Tongues*.

First boil, then blanch and spit your Tongues, season them with a little Pepper and Salt, then dip them in Eggs, throw over them a few bread crumbs and broil them 'till they are brown; serve them up with a little Gravy and Butter.

For broiling *Beef-Steaks*.

Beat your Steaks with a Rolling-pin, put pepper and salt over them, lay them on a Gridiron over a clear fire, set your Dish over a Chafing-dish of Coals, with a little brown Gravy, chop an Onion or Shalot as small as possible, and put it amongst the Gravy, if your Steaks be not over much done, Gravy will come from them, put them in your Dish all together. Garnish the Dish with Shalots and Pickles.

To broil *Fish*.

First throw Salt over them, and having drained them, dash a little flour over them, lay them upon a Cloth, and another Cloth above them, and being pretty dry, rub the Gridiron with Chalk, and put it upon the fire, which though clear, must not be too brisk, and turn your Fish frequently whilst broiling, else they will all break when you take them off.

To broil *Chubs*.

When you have scalded the Chub, cut off his Tail and Fins, wash him clean, and slit him through the Middle: Then cut him three or four times on the Back, and broil it over Charcoal, while it is broiling baste it with Butter, mingled with Salt and some Thyme shred fine.

F.

For broiling *Whitings*.

Wash them with Salt and Water and dry them well, then flour them; rub your Gridiron with Chalk for that will keep the Fish from sticking, and make it hot, then lay them on and when they are enough serve them with Oyster or Shrimp sauce. Garnish with Lemon sliced.

For broiling *Cod-founds*.

Let them lie a few Minutes in hot Water, take them out and wash them well with Salt, take off the black Dirt and skin: when they look white, put them in Water and give them a boil, take them out, flour, salt and Pepper them well, and broil them whole, when they are enough lay them in your Dish, and pour melted butter and Mustard over them.

To make *Fish Sauce*.

You must take half a pint of white Wine, be sure it is not sweet, put in it a few Cloves, Pepper, Mace, Ginger and Nutmeg, a little bunch of sweet Herbs, sweet Marjoram, Thyme, Winter Savory and one Onion, simmer it one quarter of an Hour then strain it off, put in half a pint of strong Gravy, but if you intend Lobster, Shrimp or Oyster sauce, you are to put a pint of either of them in, and stew them a quarter of an Hour; then thicken it with half a Pound of Butter and flour, made as if it were to be a Paste, and at last squeze in it some Lemon.

☞ Boil your Lobster a quarter of an Hour, whether it be for eating or for sauce.

Frying

FRYING,

How to fry *Beef Steaks*.

PEPPER and Salt your Rump Steaks or any other tender part of the Beef, and then put them in a Pan with a piece of Butter and an Onion, over a slow fire close cover'd, and as the Gravy draws, pour it from the Beef, still adding more butter at times, till your Beef is enough, then pour in your Gravy, with a Glass of strong Beer or Claret, then let it just boil up, and serve it hot with Juice of Lemon or a little Verjuice.

To fry *Beef Steaks* with *Oysters*.

Pepper some tender Beef steaks to your mind, but don't Salt them for that will make them hard; turn them often till they are enough, which you will know by their feeling firm; then salt them to your Mind.

For sauce take Oysters with their liquor, and wash them in Salt and Water, let the Oyster liquor stand and settle, then pour off the clear, stew them gently in it with a little Nutmeg or Mace, some whole Pepper, a Clove or two, and take care you don't stew them too much, for that will make them hard. when they are almost enough add a little white Wine, and a piece of butter rolled in flour to thicken it.

Some chuse to put an Anchovy, or Mushroom Ketchup into this sauce, which makes it very rich.

How to fry *Mutton Steaks.*

Cut off the Rump end of the Loin, then cut the rest into steaks and flat them with a Cleaver or Rolling-pin, season them with a little Salt and Pepper, and fry them in butter over a brisk fire, as you fry them, put them into an earthen pot till you have fried them all, then pour the fat out of the Pan, put in a little Gravy and the Gravy that comes from the steaks with a spoonful of red Wine, an Anchovy, and an Onion or a Shalot shred, shake up the steaks in the Gravy, and thicken it with Horse-raddish and shallots.

Another way of dressing *Mutton Steaks.*

First take a handfull of grated bread, a little Thyme, Parsley and Lemon-peal shred very small with some Salt, Pepper and Nut-meg; then cut a Loin of Mutton into steaks, and let them be well beaten and take the Yolks of two Eggs, rub all over the steak, strew on the grated bread with these Ingredients mix'd together and fry them. Make your sauce of gravy with a spoonful or two of Claret and some Anchovy.

For frying *Veal Cutlets.*

Cut your Veal into slices and lard them with bacon, and season them with sweet Marjoram, Nutmeg, Pepper, Salt and a little grated Lemon-peal wash them over with an Egg, and strew over them this Mixture; then fry them in sweet Butter, and serve them with Lemon sliced and Gravy.

Another

Another way of dreſſing *Veal Cutlets*.

Cut a Neck of Veal into ſteaks and fry it in Butter, boil the Scrag to ſtrong broth, add two Anchovies, two Nutmegs, ſome Lemon-peel, Penny-royal and Parſley ſhred very ſmall, burn a bit of butter, pour in the Liquor and the Veal Cutlets with a Glaſs of white Wine, and toſs them all up together. If it be not thick enough flour a bit of butter and throw in. Lay it into the Diſh, ſqueze an Orange and ſtrew as much ſalt as will reliſh.

Frying *Calves Feet* in Butter.

Blanch the Feet, boil them as you would do for eating, take out the large bones and cut them in two, beat a ſpoonful of Wheat-flour and four Eggs together, put to it a little Nutmeg, Pepper and Salt, dip in your Calves Feet and fry them in butter a light brown, and lay them upon a Diſh with melted butter over them. Garniſh your Diſh with ſlices of Lemon and ſerve them up.

To fry a Coaſt of *Lamb*.

Take a Coaſt of Lamb and par-boil it, take out all the bones as near as you can, and take four or five Yolks of Eggs beaten ſome Thyme and ſweet Marjoram, and Parſley minced very ſmall, and beat it with the Eggs, and cut your Lamb into ſquare pieces, and dip them into the Eggs and Herbs and fry them in butter, then take ſome butter white Wine and ſugar for ſauce.

How to fry *Oyſters*.

Mix a batter of flour, Milk and Eggs, then waſh your Oyſters and wipe them dry, then dip them in the

the batter, and roll them in some Crumbs of bread and a little Mace beat fine, and fry them in very hot butter or lard.

How to fry *Pancakes*.

Take a Pint of Milk or Cream, eight Eggs, a Nutmeg grated and a little Salt, then melt a pound of butter and a little Sack before you stir it, it must be as thick with flour as ordinary butter and fried with lard, turn it on the back side of a plate. Garnish with Orange and strew sugar over it.

How to make *Apple* Fritters.

Take the whites of three Eggs and the Yolks of six beat well together, and put to them a pint of Milk or Cream, then put to it four or five spoonfuls of flour, a glass of Brandy, half a Nutmeg grated and a little Ginger and Salt, the batter must be pretty thick, then slice your Apples, in rounds, dipping each round in batter, fry them in good lard over a quick Fire.

For making an *Apple Tansey*.

Cut three or four Pippins into thin slices, and fry them in good butter, then beat four Eggs with six spoonfuls of Cream, a litte Rose-water, Sugar and Nutmeg, let it fry a little and turn it with a Pie-plate. Garnish with Lemon and sugar strew'd over it.

For making a *Gooseberry Tansey*.

Fry a Quart of Gooseberrys till tender in fresh butter and mash them; then beat seven or eight Eggs, four or five Whites, a pound of sugar; three spoonfuls of Sack, as much Cream, a penny
loaf

loaf grated and three spoonfuls of flour, mix all these together, and put the Gooseberrys out of the pan to them, and stir all well together, and put them into a sauce-pan to thicken, then put fresh butter into the Frying-pen. fry them brown; and strew sugar on the top.

For making a *Water Tansey*.

Take a Dozen Eggs, and eight or nine of the Whites, beat them very well, and grate a penny-loaf, put in a quarter of a pound of melted butter and a pint of the juice of Spinnage. Sweeten it to your Taste,

For making *Apple Froise*.

Cut your Apples into thin slices, then fry them of a light brown; take them up and lay them to drain and keep them from breaking, then make the following batter: Take five Eggs, but three Whites, beat them up with flour and Cream, and a little Sack: make it the thickness of a pancake batter, pour in a little melted butter, Nutmeg and some sugar. Melt your butter, and pour batter and lay a slice of Apple here and there, pour more batter on them, fry them of a fine light brown, then take them up, and strew double refined sugar over them,

To Fry FISH.

WHEN you fry any Fish, first dip them in Yolks of Eggs, and fry them in a stew-pan over a stove, and that will make them of a Gold Colour.

White sauces are more generaly used than brown which is done chieflly by Cream, and add a little Champaign or French white Wine, and butter kneaded in flour.

To fry *Eals*.

Strip them, take out the bones and cut them in pieces, lay them for about two Hours in salt, pepper, Bay-leaves, sliced Onion, Vinegar, and the juice of Lemon, then flour them well and fry them in melted butter, and serve them, Garnish the Dish as you please.

FRICASEYS.

For making a Fricasey of *Chickens*.

FIRST half boil your Chickens, take them up, then cut them in pieces and put them in a frying-pan, and fry them in butter, then take them out of the pan and clean it, and put in some white Wine, some strong broth, some grated Nutmeg, a little Pepper and salt, a bunch of sweet Herbs, and a Shalot or two; let these with two

or

or three Anchovies stew on a slow Fire, and boil them up, then beat it with Butter and Eggs till it is thick, then put in your Chickens and toss them up well together, lay sippets in the Dish, and serve it up with sliced Lemon and fryed Parsley,

Another Way.

Take three Chickens about six Months old, flea them and cut them into pieces, and put them into your Stew-pan, with as much Gravy and Water as will cover them, put in two Anchovies well wash'd some white Pepper, Salt, and a blade of Mace, a small Onion and a few Cloves; set them to stew over a gentle Fire, and when they are enough take them from the liquor and fry them in Vinegar, but a very little; strain the liquor and take as much of it as you shall want for sauce: put to it a little Parsley, Thyme and Sorrel, boiled green and shred fine, half a Pint of sweet Cream, two yolks of Eggs well beaten, some grated Nutmeg; shake them all over the Fire, 'till 'tis thick, add to it half a Pound of Butter, and shake it well together and serve it up.

For making a brown Fricassee of Chickens.

Skin them first, then cut them in pieces, and fry them in Butter or Lard; when they are fry'd take them out and let them drain; then make forcemeat Balls and fry them: then take some strong Gravy a Shallot or two, a bunch of sweet Herbs, a little Anchovy liquor, some Spice, a glass of Claret, some thin lean Tripe cut with a Jagging-iron, to imitate Cox-combs; thicken your sauce

G   with

with burnt Butter, then put in your Chickens, and toss them up together. Garnish with fry'd Mushrooms, dipped in Butter or Parsley fried, or sliced Lemon.

For Fricasseeing Calves Feet white.

Boil the Feet as you would do for eating, then take out the Bones, and cut them in two, put them in a Stew-pan, with a little white Gravy, and a Spoonful or two of white Wine, take the yolks of two or three Eggs, two or three Spoonfuls of Cream, grate a little Nutmeg and Salt, with a lump of Butter, shake all well together. Garnish your Dish with slices of Lemon and Currants, then serve it up.

A white Fricassee of Chickens.

Either half roast or parboil your Chickens, then skin them and cut them in pieces, stew them in strong Broth, some Pepper and a blade of Mace, with a little Salt, two Anchovies, and a small Onion, let it stew till it is tender, then take out your Onion and put in a quarter of a Pint of Cream, a piece of Butter work'd up in Flour, and stir it over the Fire till all is as thick as Cream, and wring in the juice of a Lemon, and be careful it do not crudle, serve on sipets and put in some Mushrooms and Oysters.

How to Fricassee Ducks.

Quarter them, and beat them with the back of your Cleaver, dry them well, fry them in sweet Butter, when they are almost fry'd, put in a handful of Onions, shred small, and a little Thyme; then put in a little Claret, thin slices of Bacon,

Spinage

Spinage and Parsley boiled green, and shred small break the yolks of three Eggs, with a little Pepper into a Dish, and some grated Nutmeg, tols them up with a ladleful of drawn Butter, pour this on your Ducks; lay your Bacon upon them, and serve them hot.

For Fricasseeing a Goose

Roast your Goose, and before it is quite done cut and scotch it with your Knife long-ways, then flash it acrols, strew Salt and Pepper over it; then fry it in your Pan with the skinny side downward till it has taken a gentle heat; then broil it on a Gridiron over a gentle Fire; when it is enough baste the upper side with Butter, a little Sugar, Vinegar and Mustard, pour this into the Dish with Sausages and Lemon, and serve it up.

To Fricassee Pigeons in their Blood.

Take some Pigeons from the Dove house, just before they are ready to fly, and bleed them to Death and save the Blood, squeeze a Lemon into it, or it will change, scald your Pigeons and cut them in Quarters; draw them and save what more Blood you can; put them into your Stew-pan, first season them with Pepper and Salt, and a faggot of sweet Herbs, add Mushrooms, Truffels, Morels, Cocks-combs, Sweet-breads, Palates and Artichoke-bottoms, and tols them all up in melted Bacon, throw in some Flour and two spoonfuls of Gravy, and make it simmer over a clear Fire, when it is enough skim off the Fat and thicken it with a Cullis; strain your Blood through a sieve, and beat it up with the Yolk of an Egg, and put in a

little

little minc'd young Parsley when you are ready, pour in the Blood and continue stirring it (and not let it boil) till hot, and serve it. Garnish it as you please.

To Fricassee Chickens and Rabbets.

Take Rabbits and Chickens and skin them; cut them into small pieces, beat them flat and lard them with Bacon, season it with Salt, Pepper and Mace; dredge it with Flour and fry it in sweet Butter to a good colour, then get the quantity of good Gravy as your Fricassee requires with Oysters and Mushrooms, two or three Anchovies and some Shallots. a bunch of sweet Herbs, and if you like it, a glass of Claret, season high; and before you put in your Meat simmer it well together till the goodness of the Herbs is out; then take out the Herbs, Shallot and Anchovy-bones, and cut a Lemon in dice and put in your Chickens or Rabbits, and let it stew gently till it be tender; but be sure to keep it stirring all the while it is over the Fire and make it as thick as Cream, serve it up with Force-meat balls, crisp Bacon and fried Oysters, garnish it as you like.

For makeing a brown Fricassee of Rabbits.

Cut your Rabbits into small pieces, then fry them in Butter over a quick Fire; when they are fry'd take them out of the Butter and heat them in a Stew-pan with a little Nutmeg, Flour and Butter, then take it up and put a few Bread-crumbs over it, season'd with Lemon-peel, Parsley, Thyme some Salt and Pepper. Garnish with crisp Parsley.

For makeing a white Fricaffee of Rabbits.

Half boil a couple of young Rabbits and when they are cold cut them in small pieces, then put them into a Stew-pan with white Gravy, a small Onion, a small Anchovy, shred Mace and Lemon-peel; set it over the stove and let it have one boil then take some Cream, the Yolks of two Eggs, a lump of Butter, shred Parfley and some juice of Lemon; put them altogether into a Stew-pan and shake them over the Fire till they are as white as Cream, you must not let it boil, if you do it will curdle. Garnish your Dish with some Pickles and Lemon.

How to Fricaffee cold roaſt Beef.

Firſt cut your Beef into very thin ſlices, then shred a handful of Parſley very ſmall, cut an Onion into pieces, and put them together in a Stew-pan with a piece of Butter, with a good quantity of ſtrong Broth, ſeaſon with Pepper and Salt, let it ſtew gently a quarter of an Hour, then beat the Yolk of four Eggs in ſome Claret and a Spoonful of Vinegar and put to your Meat, ſtirring it till it grows thick, rub your Diſh with a Shallot before you ſerve it up.

To Fricaffee Veal.

Cut your Veal in thin ſlices, beat it well with a Rolling-pin, then ſeaſon it with Pepper, Salt, Nutmeg, Thyme and Lemon-peel, shred very ſmall; fry it in Butter, and when it is enough as it will be in ſix Minutes, pour away the Butter it is fry'd in and throw in freſh, with two Eggs well beaten,

and

and two Spoonfuls of Verjuice; shake it up altogether, and then serve it up.

Parboil your Meat that is used for Fricassees, for stewing them too long on the Fire will make them hard.

To make a Fricassee of Lamb.

Cut a hind Quarter of Lamb into thin slices, season them with Savoury, Spice, sweet Herbs, and a Shalot; then fry them, and toss them up in strong Broth, white Wine, Oysters, two Palates, a little brown Butter, forced meat balls, or an Egg or two to thicken it, or a bit of Butter roll'd in Flour. Garnish with sliced Lemon.

Another Way.

Lamb must be cut into small pieces; then seasoned with a little Pepper and Salt, fryed first in Water, and after being well floured in Butter; it requires a longer Time than Veal. When enough done pour off that Butter, and put fresh, with two Eggs, and very little Verjuice, strew it in the Dish with Mushrooms,

Fricassee of Eggs.

Boil ten or twelve Eggs hard, cut them in quarters and put them into a Pint of strong Gravy, and a quarter of a Pint of white Wine; season them with Cloves, Mace, Pepper and Salt, and boil a little Spinage to colour them green, with a few Mushrooms and Oysters, and stew it a little while gently; thicken it with a piece of Butter and the Yolk of an Egg, and a little Flour all rolled together, and make it thick, serve it with crisp sippets, Lemon and fry'd Parsley.

Directions

Directions for HASHING.

For hashing a Calves Head.

SLIT your Calves Head, cleanse and half boil it, and when it is cold, cut it in thin slices, and fry it in a Pan of brown Butter; then put it in a Stew-pan over a Stove, with a Pint of Gravy, as much strong Broth, a quarter of a Pint of Claret, as much white Wine, and a Handful of savory Balls, two or three shrivelled Palates, a Pint of Oysters, Cocks-combs, Lamb-stones, and Sweet-breads, boiled, blanched and sliced with Mushrooms and Truffles; then put your Hash in the Dish, and the other Things, some round it, and some on it. Garnish your Dish with sliced Lemon.

Another Way.

Boil the Head till the Meat is near enough for eating, take it up and cut it into thin slices; then put to it half a pint of good Gravy: To this Liquor put two Anchovies, half a Nutmeg, a little Mace, and a small Onion stuck with Cloves. boil this up in the Liquor a quarter of an Hour; then strain it and let it boil gently again. then put in your Meat with a little Salt. and some Lemon-peel shred fine and let it stew a little: Mix the Brains with the Yolks of Eggs, and fry them for Garnish when the Head is ready, shake in a piece of Butter and serve it up.

For hashing Beef.

Cut some tender Beef into slices, and put them in a Stew-pan, well floured with a slice of Butter over a quick Fire, for three Minutes. and then add a little Water, a bunch of sweet Herbs, some Lemon-peel, an Onion, or a little Marjoram, with Pepper, Salt and grated Nutmeg; cover them close, and let them stew till they are tender, then put in a glass of Claret, or strong Beer, and then strain your sauce; serve it hot, and garnish with Lemon sliced and Beet-root. This is a very good Dish.

To hash Chickens.

Cut six Chickens into quarters, cover them almost with Water, and season them with Salt, Pepper. a handful of shred Parsley, half a Pint of white Wine; when they are boiled enough, add these to the Yolks of six Eggs, with a little Nutmeg, Vinegar and Ketchup, and a good piece of Butter; warm all these together, and pour them into a Soop-dish and serve them up.

For hashing a Leg of Mutton.

Half roast a Leg of Mutton, and when it is cold cut it in thin pieces as you would do any other Meat for hashing, then put it into a Stew-pan, with a little Water or small Gravy, two or three Spoonfuls of red Wine, two or three Shalots, or Onions, and two or three Spoonfuls of Oyster Pickle; thicken it with a little Flour, and so serve it up. Garnish the Dish with Horse Raddish and Pickles.

You may do a shoulder of Mutton the same Way, only boil the Blade-bone, and let it lie in the middle.

For hashing any Part of Mutton.

Cut the Mutton into very small pieces, and then take about half a Pint of Oysters, and after washing them in Water, put them in their own Liquor in a Sauce-pan, with some whole Pepper, Mace, and a little Salt; when they have stewed a little put in a Spoonful of Ketchup and an Anchovy, or pickled Wallnut liquor, some Gravy, or Water; then put in your Mutton, and a piece of Butter rolled in Flour; then let it boil till the Mutton is warm through, then add a glass of Claret; lay it upon sipets. Garnish with sliced Lemon or Capers, and if you please some Mushrooms, then serve it up.

Another Way of hashing Mutton, or any such Meat.

Take a little whole Pepper, Salt, a few sprigs of sweet Herbs, a little Anchovy, one Shallot, two slices of Lemon, or a little Broth or Water; let it stew a little, and thicken it with burnt Butter. Serve it with Pickles and Sipets.

Directions for STEWING.

An exceeding good Way to stew Chickens.

TAKE Chickens, flee them and cut them in pieces cross-way, then put them in a Pipkin

kin or Skillet, and cover them almoſt with Pepper Mace, and Water, ſo let them ſtew ſoftly with a whole Onion in it, till part of the liquor be conſumed, then put in as much white Wine as will cover them again, take Parſley, ſweet Marjoram winter Savory with ſome Thyme, and ſhred them very ſmall and put them in, let them boil till they are almoſt enough, then put in a good piece of Butter.

For ſtewing Ducks whole.

Draw your Ducks, and waſh them clean; then put them into a Stew-pan, with ſtrong Broth, an Anchovy, Lemon-peel, whole Pepper, an Onion Mace and red Wine; when well ſtewed, put in a piece of Butter, and ſome grated Bread to thicken it; lay ſome Meat Balls and criſped Bacon round them. Garniſh with Shalots.

To ſtew wild Fowls.

Roaſt them till half enough, and cut them in pieces; ſet them over a Chaffing-diſh or Charcoal with half a Pint of Claret, and the ſame quantity of Beef-gravy, firſt boil'd and ſeaſon'd with Spice and Shalot; ſtew it in this liquor till high colour'd and well mix'd, then ſerve it up.

To ſtew a Green Gooſe.

Cut your Gooſe in two and put it in a Stew-pan; and at the bottom put Lards of Bacon and Beef, with Onions, Savory, Thyme and Marjoram, with Carrots, ſlices of Lemon, Pepper, Cloves and Salt: Put it over a good Charcoal Fire till enough, often turning it; then make a Ragoo of Green Geeſe toſs'd up with a little freſh Butter and Flour, a bunch of ſweet Herbs, Salt and Pepper

moillen

moisten it with Gravy; and when you serve it thicken it with the yolks of two Eggs, beat it in Cream. Dish up your Goose and pour the Ragoo upon it.

This Ragoo serves for a Breast of Veal, or Pigeons stewed

For stewing Pigeons.

Season and stuff your Pigeons, flat the Breast-bone and truss them up as you would do for baking. dredge them over with some Flour, and fry them in Butter, turning them round till all sides be brown; then put them into a Stew-pan, with as much Gravy as will cover them and let them stew till they are done; then take part of the Gravy, an Anchovy shred, a small Onion or a Shallot, a little juice of Lemon for sauce; pour it over your Pigeons, and lay round them Forced-meat Balls and crisp Bacon. Garnish your Dish with Lemon and crisp Parsley.

To stew Pigeons white.

Take twelve Pigeons with their Giblets and quarter them, put them in a Stew-pan, with just Water sufficient to stew them without burning; let your Fire be clear and not fierce; when they are tender thicken the liquor with the yolks of two Eggs, six or seven spoonfuls of sweet Cream, a little Butter a little shred Thyme and Parsley; shake them all together, and garnish it with sliced Lemon.

Giblets Stew'd.

Parboil them and toss them up in a Stew-pan as a Fricassee. and put into your Pan some strong Broth cover them close and let them stew gently, till the

Broth is near wasted: In the mean Time take two French Rolls and let them simmer in strong Broth, and when ready to serve place them in the middle of your Dish, and lay your Giblets upon them, and round them; then pour in some Mutton Gravy made thus: Half roast your Meat, then pick it and squeeze it in a Press to force the Gravy out: Then take two Spoonfuls of strong Broth, and wet your Meat with it, then press it again; Salt it well and keep it in an earthen Pot, and use it as you want it.

For stewing Rabbits.

Cut them into quarters, then lard them with pretty large Lardoons of Bacon, fry them and put them in a Stew-pan, with strong Broth, white Wine, Pepper, Salt, a Faggot of sweet Herbs, fried Flour and Orange.

For stewing a Pig.

First roast the Pig till it is hot; then take off the Skin and cut it in pieces; then put it in a Stew-pan, with good Gravy and white Wine, some Pepper, Salt, Nutmeg, and an Onion, and a little sweet Marjoram, a little elder Vinegar, and some Butter, and when it is stewed enough then lay it upon sipets, and garnish the Dish with sliced Lemon.

For stewing Beef.

Brisket-beef, Thick-flank, or the Chuck-rib, are the best for stewing; cut it in Pieces of about four or five Ounces each; put it into an earthen Pipkin, with a few Turnips, one Carrot, one whole Onion, a little Thyme, Winter-savoury,

sweet

sweet Marjoram, Parsley, some Corns of Jamaica Pepper, Salt and black Pepper, three or four Bay-leaves; then put as much Water as will a little more than cover them; stop it very close to keep the steem as much as possible from going out, and set it over a slow Fire, so that it may just simmer: If it be a brisket, it will take full four Hours to do it right; if any other part, three Hours will be quite sufficient. When it is enough, take out the Bay-leaves, and serve up the rest altogether in a soop Dish.

For stewing a Rump of Beef.

Take a fat Rump of young Beef, lard the low part with fat Bacon, cut off the Fag-end, and stuff the other part with shred Parsley, put it into the Pan with a quart of red Wine, two or three Quarts of Water, two or three Anchovies, some whole Pepper, a bunch of sweet Herbs, an Onion, two or three blades of Mace: stew it over a slow Fire five or six Hours, turning it several Times in the stewing, and keep it close cover'd; when your Beef is stewed enough take the Gravy from it, thicken it with a lump of Butter and Flour, put it upon a Dish with the Beef. Garnish the Dish with Horse-radish and Beet-root; there must be no Salt upon the Beef, only salt the Gravy to your Taste.

You may stew part of a Brisket or an Ox-cheek, the same Way.

For stewing Beef Collops.

Take some raw Beef and cut it in the same manner as you do Veal for Scotch Collops; lay it in the pan

pan with a little Water, put to it some Pepper and Salt, some Morjoram powdered, a Gill of white Wine and a slice or two of fat Bacon, and some flour'd Butter, put it over a quick Fire for a little Time 'till cover'd with Gravy, you may put in a little Ketchup, serve it hot and garnish with sliced Lemon.

To stew Beef-Steaks.

Take the Steaks of a Rib. and half broil them, put them into your Stew-pan cover'd with Gravy; let them be well season'd with Pepper and Salt; roll up a bit of Butter and Flour and the yolk of an Egg and throw it in; serve it in with a few Capers thrown over it.

To stew a Neck, Breast, Knuckle, or any other Joint of Veal.

Whatever Joint of Veal is to stew, must be put whole into the Stew-pan, with Parsley, Winter-savory, sweet Marjoram, Thyme, Lemon-peel, Mace, Nutmeg, a little Salt and Pepper; mix some white Wine in the Water, and put no more than will just cover it; then stop it close and put it over a very slow Fire: When it is enough, beat up the Yolks of three or four Eggs, and incorporate them with the Gravy that comes from it and when you have put it in the Dish, strew a few Mushrooms, Capers, and a little Samphire over, and garnish with Lemon or Seville Orange. You may also add Truffles, Morelles, Coxcombs, and Artichoke-bottoms if you have them. This is

a very

a very delicate and favoury Difh and pleafes moft palates.

For ftewing Veal.

Take fome lean Veal, either roafted or boiled; cut it into thick Slices, with Water juft to cover them, then put a little Mace and Nutmeg, a little Pepper and Salt, a Shalot, a little Lemon-peel and fweet Marjoram; when they are ftewed near enough put fome Mufhroom Gravy into the Liquor, a glafs of white Wine, fome Lemon-juice, and let it ftew a little longer, then ftrain off the Liquor, and you may put fome Mufhrooms in the fauce, and thicken your fauce with Cream or Butter rolled in Flour. Garnifh with fliced Lemon or Orange, and fried Oyfters.

To ftew a Neck or Breaft of Mutton.

Some People like Mutton ftewed with Potatoes; and if fo, you muft cut the Mutton into Chops and flice your Potatoes, put in a larger quantity of Salt and Pepper than you do either with Beef or Veal, and a very little Water, becaufe what comes from the Potatoes when they have been a little Time on the Fire will ftew the Mutton. Put in no Herbs except a bunch of Thyme, and covering it clofe, let it juft fimmer an Hour and a half, but let no fteam evaporate. To ftew Mutton without Potatoes, you muft alfo cut the Chops or Collops, according as the part is, and put in two or three Turnips, Thyme, Parfley, Salt, Pepper a fmall Onion, and as much Water as will cover it, and when done ftrew it over with fome Capers.

For stewing a Rump or Leg of Mutton.

After breaking the Bones, put them in a Pot with a little Mace, Salt and whole Pepper, an Anchovy, Nutmeg, a Turnip, two Onions, a little bunch of sweet Herbs, a pint of Ale, a Quart of Claret, a Quart or two of Water, and a hard Crust of Bread; stop it up and let it stew five Hours, and serve it with Toasts and the Gravy.— You may do an Ox-cheek in the same Manner.

For stewing Mutton Chops.

Cut them thin, take two earthen Pans and put one over the other, lay them between, and burn brown Paper under them.

To stew Sausages.

Boil them in fair Water and Salt a small Time, for sauce boil some Currants alone, when they be almost tender, then pour out the Water and put in some white Wine, Butter and Sugar.

For stewing a Carp.

Take half Claret and half Gravy, as much as will cover your Carp in the Pan, with Mace, whole Pepper, a few Cloves, two Anchovies, a little Horse-radish, a Shalot or Onion and some Salt; when the Carp is enough, take it out and boil the Liquor as fast as possible till it be just enough to make sauce; flour a bit of Butter, and throw it into it, squeeze the juice of one Lemon, and pour it over the Carp.

For stewing Trout,

Wash a large Trout, and put it in a Pan with white Wine and Gravy, then take two Eggs buttered, some Salt, Pepper, Nutmeg and Lemon-peel

peel, some grated Bread, and a little Thyme, mix all together and put in the belly of the Trout, then let it stew a quarter of an Hour, and put a piece of butter into the sauce; serve it hot and garnish with Lemon sliced.

For stewing *Cod*.

Cut your Cod in thin slices, and lay it at the bottom of your Pan with half a pint of white Wine, a pint of gravy and some Oysters and some Liquor, pepper, salt and some Nutmeg, and let it stew till it is near enough, then thicken it with a piece of Butter rolled in flour, let it stew a little longer, then serve it hot, and garnish with Lemon sliced.

To stew *Crabs*.

Take out the Meat and cleanse it from the skins, put it into a Stew-pan, with a quarter of a Pint of white wine, some Crumbs of white Bread an Anchovy and a little Nutmeg, set them over a gentle Charcoal Fire, with the Yolk of an Egg beat into it, some pepper, and stir all together and serve them up.

For stewing *Oysters*.

First wash them in clear water, then set on some of their own Liquor, Water and white Wine, a blade of Mace and some whole Pepper, let it boil very well, then put in your Oysters, and let them just boil up, thicken them with the Yolks of two Eggs, a piece of butter and some flour beat up very well, thicken it and serve it up with Sippets and Lemons.

For stewing *Pike*.

Scale and clean a large Pike, season it in the belly with some salt and Mace, skewer it round, put it into a deep stew-pan with a pint of small gravy, a pint of red Wine and two or three blades of Mace, set it over a stove with a slow fire, and cover it up close, put into it two Anchovies and some Lemon peal shred fine, and thicken the sauce with Butter; before you lay the Pike on the Dish, turn it with the back upwards, take off the skin and serve it up, garnish the Dish with Lemon and Pickle.

To stew *Tench*.

Cut your Tench and wash them clean, fry them in brown butter, then stew them with white Wine, Verjuice, a faggot of sweet Herbs, Salt, Pepper, Nutmeg, a Bay-leaf and some Flour. When the Fish is enough put in some Oysters, Capers, Ketchup and some Lemon. Garnish your Dish with crisp Bread.

Another Way.

Scale and gut a live Tench and wash the inside with Vinegar, then put it into a stew-pan, when the Water boils, with some salt, a bunch of sweet Herbs, some Lemon-peal, and whole pepper; cover it up close and boil it quick till enough, then strain off some of the Liquor, and put to it some white Wine and Walnut Liquor, or Mushroom Gravy, an Anchovy and some Oysters and Shrimps, boil these together and toss them up with thick butter rolled in flour, adding some Lemon juice.

Garnish

Garnish with Lemon and Horse-raddish, serve it hot with sippets.

To stew *Carp* an admirable Way.

Scrape and gut them, put them into a Stew-pan with the Blood and half a Pint of white Wine Vinegar, and as much Claret as will cover them, with a bundle of sweet Herbs, one Onion, two or three Anchovies and Jamaica Pepper, set them over a Charcoal fire and let them stew gently, you must stir them two or three Times: When you are ready take them up out of the Liquor into a Dish, and keep them hot; then put in half a pound of butter, and the Yolks of two Eggs, and some Mushrooms, and shake it over the fire to thicken, then pour it over the Fish. If you please you may leave out the Blood, and put in Oysters and Shrimps.

To Butter *Lobsters*.

Take out all the Meat and put it into a Sauce-pan with some season'd Gravy, some Vinegar and drawn Butter, and set it over the Fire a small time, then fill your Shells and put the rest in small plates.

To stew a *Pike* with *Oysters*.

First Scale and gut it and wash it clean; Cut it in Pieces and put it into a Stew-pan, with white Wine, Parsley, Cives, Mushrooms and Truffels, all of them hash'd together with Salt, Pepper and Butter and set over a stove to stew; blanch some Oysters in Water, and some Verjuice: Throw them with their own Liquor into the Stew-pan, when the Pike is near enough, when done serve it: Garnish your Dish with sliced Lemon.

A Pudding for the belly of a *Pike*.

Take Crumbs of bread finely grated, work'd up in a Lump of butter, and seasoned with an Anchovy finely shred, a small Onion shred, and some sweet Herbs, with some grated Nutmeg and the Liver of the Fish.

Note, The Liver is not always put in.

To dress *Smelts*.

Let them stew in a pan with butter, white Wine a piece of Lemon, some flour and Nutmeg, and serve them up with Capers.

To make a good sauce for all fresh *Fish*.

Take two Anchovies, and boil them in some white Wine, a quarter of an Hour with a Shalot cut thin; then melt your butter very thick, and put in a pint of pick'd shrimps, and give them a heat in the butter, and pour them upon the Fish: You may add Oyster Liquor if you will.

The following curious Receipt for dressing a Turtle, having been much enquiered after, was receiv'd from a Cook in the Indias, where they are dressed to the utmost Perfection.

How to clean and dress a *Turtle*.

YOU must first cut off the Head, and hang the Turtle up by one of the hindmost Fins, that the Blood may run from it to make the Fish white.

white. This done, cut off the Fins and wash them clean; then cut of the belly shell well with Meat, take out the Guts and wash them very clean, and observe you turn them the right way, or else you will meat with a great deal of Trouble. Stew the Guts with a Quart or three Pints of the best Madeira Wine, infuse half a Dram of Coyn butter. Then having boiled the four Fins, and took the Scales off, stew them with the Guts on the belly part called the Collop. Put all sorts of the best of sweet Herbs cut or shred very small, and strew them over the Collop. Put pieces of the rest butter, one Bottle of the best Madeira Wine, and strew a Dram and a half of your Pepper, or Coyn butter over it. Take great care it is not over baked. You may cut off Collops and dress them as Veal Cutlets. Send your Guts up in the top shell and set it at the upper end of the Table; the Collops in the Middle, and at the lower End, which garnish with the four Fins.

This is the properest Way of dressing this Fish in any part of the Indias or England, approved by the best and most experienced Cooks who undertake to dress them.

To stew *Snipes*.

First slit and wash them, but take nothing out of their bellies, toss them up in a stew pan over a clear fire with some melted bacon, season them to your palate with Pepper and Salt; pour in some Ketchup, and when they are enough squeze in the Juice of a Quarter of a Lemon, garnish them with Lemon-peel sliced and serve them.

A

A Ragoo of *Snipes*.

Cut them in four and tofs them up in melted bacon and butter, but let all their entrails remain with them, feafon them with Pepper, Salt and the Juice of Mufhrooms, and ftew it together till it is done; then fqueeze in a Lemon or Orange, and ferve them up.

FORCE-MEATS, &c.

Forc'd Meat, to be ufed as occafion requires.

TAKE four pound of a Leg or Fillet of Veal and two pound of fat bacon, two pound of good Suet; boil them over a clear fire three Quarters of an Hour, and throw them into cold Water, leaft your fat bacon fhould diffolve in mincing; Mince all thefe very fine, each feperate and then all together take the Crumb of four French Rolls foaked in Milk; fixteen Eggs raw, Pepper, Salt, Onion and Parfley according to your pallate, half a Nutmeg, and put all them with the above Ingredients into a Mortar and pound them very fine, and keep it for your Ufe: This may be ufed with moft Difhes; indeed in Pies Eggs are not proper.

To make *Forc'd Meat Balls*.

Take a pound of Veal and the fame Wheight of beef fuet and a bit of bacon, fhred all together, beat it in a Mortar very fine, then feafon it with
some

some sweet Herbs, Pepper, Salt, Cloves, Mace and some Nutmeg; and when you roll it up to fry then add the Yolks of two or three Eggs to bind it, you may add Oysters or Marrow at an Entertainment.

Another Way.

Take Half a pound of suet, as much Veal cut fine and beat in a marble Mortar or wooden Bowl, have a few sweet Herbs shred fine and some Mace dried and beat fine, a small Nutmeg grated or half a large one, some pepper, salt and the Yolks of two Eggs, mix all these well together and roll them in flour and fry them brown. If they are for any thing of white sauce, put some Water on in a sauce-pan, and when the Water boils, put them in and let them boil for a few Minutes; but never fry them for a white sauce.

Chickens Forc'd with Oysters.

Lard and truss them; make a forcing of Oysters, sweet-breads, Parsley, Truffels, Mushrooms and some Onions, chop these together and season it; mix it with a piece of butter, a Yolk of an Egg, and tie them at both Ends and rost them: Make for them a Ragoo, and garnish with sliced Lemon.

An exceeding good Way of dressing Chickens.

Take out the breasts, lard them and force them with forc'd Meat. Stew them in a pan and Dish them; Let your sauce be butter not too thick, Gravy and shred parsley.

Of POTTING.

To Pott *Beef*.

TAKE a good Buttock of Beef, and take out the bone and lay it flat and flash it in several places, then salt it well and let it lie in salt three Days; then take it out and let it lie in the running Water, with a Handful of salt three Days longer, then take it out, and dry it with a Cloth and season it with Pepper, salt, Nutmeg, Cloves, Mace, and two ounces of Salt-petre finely beaten, then shred two or three pounds of beef-suet and a pound of Butter, put some in the bottom of the pot you bake it in, then put in your beef and the rest of the butter and suet on the Top: cover your pot over with coarse paste and set it in all Night with Houshold bread, in the Morning draw it and pour off all the Fat and Lean, and work it into your pots that you keep in while it is hot, or it will not close so well, then cover it with the clear fat you poured off, paper it when cold, it will keep good a Month or six Weeks.

For potting a *Hare*.

Bone your Hare and take away all the skinny part, then put to the flesh some good fat bacon, and savory Herbs, season it with Nutmeg and pepper, and some salt, then beat all this fine in a Mortar and pot it down, put in a pint of Claret and bake it about an Hour and a Half, and when it it comes out pour out all the Gravy and fill it up with clarify'd butter.

For potting *Tongues*.

Take two Tongues and salt them with salt-petre white salt, brown sugar: bake them tender in Pump Water, then blanch them and cut off the roots. and season with pepper and spice, put them in an oval Pot and cover them all over with clarified butter.

Another Way.

Take Neat's Tongues, and rub them very well with Salt and Water (bay salt is best) then take Pump Water with a good deal of Salt-petre and some white Salt, some Cloves and Mace, and boil it well and scum it. when it is cold put your Tongues in and let them lie in it six Days; then wash them out of the Liquor and put them in a Pot, and bake them with Bread till they are very tender, and when they are taken out of the Oven pull off their Skins. and put them in the Pot you intend to keep them in. and cover them over with clarified Butter, They will keep four or five Months.

For potting *Mutton*.

Take a Leg of Mutton, of twelve Pounds. and cut into pound pieces, salt it as for a Collar of Beef. let it lie six Days, bake it in a Pan cover'd with Pump Water, and bake it with Houshold bread, when it comes out of the Oven take it out of the Liquor and beat it in a Stone Mortar, then season it with an Ounce of Pepper half an Ounce of Cloves and Mace; mix into it an Ounce of clarified butter,

K put

put it close into your pot and cover it with clarified Butter on the top half an Inch thick.

For potting *Cheshire Cheese*.

Put three Pound of Cheshire Cheese into a Mortar and a pound of the best fresh Butter you can get; pound them together, and in the beating add a glass or two of Canary, and half an Ounce of Mace, so finely beaten and sifted that it cannot be discerned. When all is well mixed press it hard down into a Pan, cover it with some melted Butter and keep it cool.

A slice of this upon Bread eats very fine.

For making white *Scotch Collops*.

Cut about four Pounds of a fillet of Veal into thin slices, take a clean Stew-pan and Butter it over, shake some flour over it, then lay your Meat in piece by piece till your pan is covered; then take three or four blades of Mace, and some Nutmeg. set your stew-pan over the Fire, toss it up together till all your Meat be white: then take half a Pint of strong Veal Broth which must be ready made, a quarter of a Pint of Cream, and the Yolks of two Eggs, mix all these well together, put it to your Meat, keeping it tossing all the while till they just boil up, when they are enough squeeze in some Lemon: You may add Oysters and Mushrooms to make it rich.

Scotch Collops an excellent Way.

Take the Flesh part of a Leg of Veal, lard it with bacon, as much as you think fit, sliced very thin, take half a Pint of Ale and do the Veal in it till the blood be out; then pour out the Ale into a Porringer

ringer and take some Thyme, Savory and sweet Marjoram, chop'd small; strew over the Veal, fry it in Butter, and Flour it a little till enough; then put it in a Dish, put the Butter away, and fry thin bits of Bacon and lay it in the middle of the Dish. For the Sauce, put into the Ale four Anchovies and some white Wine, the Yolks of two Eggs, some Nutmeg. Melt the Anchovies before you put in the Eggs, when it begins to thicken put in a piece of Butter and shake it about till melted; then pour it over your Meat. You may do it in Gravy instead of Ale, melt your Anchovies in white Wine.

Of RAGOOS.

For ragooing *Lamb Stones.*

HAVING got two or three pair of Lamb-stones, par-boil them, take off the Skin, and cut them in four or eight Pieces, strew some fine Salt over them and wipe them dry; flour them without touching them with your Hands, fry them immediately in very hot Hog's-lard, and make them crisp; then Dish them up and serve away.

For ragooing a *Breast of Veal.*

Lard a breast of Veal, and half roast it, then pour strong Gravy upon, and stew it very well with a bunch of sweet Herbs, an Onion, Pepper and Salt, Cloves and Mace; then for Sauce, take

some

some Butter and brown it, shake some Flour into it take the Liquor you stew'd your Veal in and boil it with Palates Oysters, Mushrooms, Forced Meat, Artichoke bottoms, and Sweet-breads, squeeze in a Lemon, and after you have strain'd off your Herbs, toss it up all together and pour it over the Veal.

A Ragoo of *Cock's Combs. Cock's Kidneys*, and fat *Livers*.

Take a Stew-pan, put in a bit of Butter, a bunch of sweet Heabs, some Mushrooms and Truffels; put it, for a Minute over the Fire, Flour it a little moisten it with half a spoonful of Broth, season it with Salt and Pepper, let it stew a little, then put in Cock's-combs, Cock's-kidneys, fat Livers and sweet-breads, let your Ragoo be Palatable, thicken it with the Yolks of Eggs, serve it hot for a dainty Dish.

For dressing *Lamb* in Ragoo.

Take your Lamb, half roast it, then cut it in four pieces, and toss it up in a Stew-pan to brown it, then stew it in good Broth, with Salt, Pepper, Cloves, a few Mushrooms and sweet Herbs; when it is enough put to it a Cullis of Veal and then serve it up.

Of COLLARING.

For Collaring *Beef*.

TAKE a thin flank of Beef, flit it through the middle, Salt it with a quarter of a Pound of Salt petre and a Quart of white Salt, let it lie fix Days. then feafon it with an Ounce of Pepper, half an Ounce of Cloves and Mace, a little Thyme and Lemon-peel finely fhred, roll it up tight, bind it hard with coarfe Tape, and cover it with Pumpwater, and then bake it in a Pan with Houfhold Bread. When it comes out of the Oven, roll it tight in a coarfe Cloth, and tie it at both Ends; when cold, take off the Cloth and Tape and keep it in a cool Place.

For Collaring a *Breaſt of Veal*.

Take a Breaſt of Veal and bone it, lay all over the infide thin flices of Bacon, feafon it with Salt, Pepper and Spice, fome Thyme, Lemon peel and Sage, roll it up into a Collar; and bind it tight with Tape, boil it in white Wine Vinegar and Water, whole Cloves and Mace, and a bunch of fweet Herbs, and a flice or two of Lemon, let it boil two Hours, keep it in the Liquor you boil it in and ferve it in flices with Oyl and Lemon.

For Collaring *Mutton*.

Take a large breaſt of Mutton, bone it and feafon it with Pepper. Salt and Spice, Thyme and Lemon

Lemon peel shred fine, roll it up tight and bind it hard with Tape, boil it two Hours in Water and Salt, with some whole Spice and Pepper and a bunch of sweet Herbs. Serve it in slices with all sorts of Pickles.

For Collaring *Pork*.

Take a belly piece of Pork, bone it and season it high in Pepper, Salt and Spice, and a good handful of Sage shred; roll it tight as before directed; boil it five Hours in the same Pickle as for the Veal before. Serve it with Mustard and some Sugar.

For Collaring *Pig*.

Take a large Pig and cut off his Head, slit him down the back, bone it. lay it in Water four Hours then dry it well, season it with Pepper, Salt and Spice and a Handful of Sage shred, Roll it all into one Collar, put it into a Cloth, tie it with coarse Tape. Boil it three Hours in white Wine Vinegar and Water, of each a like Quantity, put in some Salt, a bunch of sweet Herbs, whole Cloves Mace and Pepper, and a slice or two of Lemon. When cold take off the Tape and Cloth, keep it in the Pickle, serve it in slices with Lemon and some of the Pickle.

For Collaring *Eals*.

Take a large Eal and split it down the Back take out the bone and season it high with Pepper, Salt, Spice, and some Thynie shred fine, roll it up into a Collar, put a Cloth about it and bind it with Tape, boil it one Hour in white Wine and Vinegar, of each a like quantity, with whole Pepper

and

and Spice and a bunch of sweet Herbs, a slice or two of Lemon with some Salt. When it is cold take off the Tape and Cloth, and keep it in the Pickle you boil it in. Serve it in slices with Oyl, Lemon and some of the Pickle.

SALTING DRYING &c.

To Salt *Hams, Tongues, &c.*

TAKE of Spanish Salt a Peck, of Salt-petre four Ounces double refin'd, five Pounds of brown Sugar; put all these to as much Water as will bear an Egg; after it is well stir'd, lay the Hams so that they're cover'd with the Pickle, let them lie three Weeks if middling Hams, if large a Month, when you take them out, dry them well in a Cloth, and rub them well with Bay Salt, then hang them up to dry, and smoke them with Saw-dust every Day for a Fortnight together, the Chimney you hang them in must be of a moderate Heat the Pickle must be raw and not boil'd. This Quantity is enough to salt six Hams at a time. When you take them out, you may take the Pickle and skim it clean putting in some fresh Salt. If you keep your Hams till they are dry and old, lay them in hot Grains and let them lie till cold, then wrap them up in Hay, and they will boil tender. set them on in cold Water when they are dry the Tongues before stopped with Salt and tyed up close in brown Paper, to keep out the Flies.——

Note

Note. *Neat's Hearts, Tongues, or Hog's Cheeks* do well in the same Pickle, the best way is to rub Hams with Bay Salt and Sugar, three or four Days before you put them in this Pickle.

Another way.

Take three or four Gallons of Water, and put to it four Pound of Bay Salt, four Pound of white Salt, a pound of Petre-salt, a Quarter of a Pound of Salt Petre, two Ounces of Prunella Salt, and a Pound of brown Sugar, let it boil a quarter of an Hour, scum it well, when it is cold, serve it from the bottom into the Vessel you keep it in.

Let Hams lie in this Pickle four or five Weeks, a Clod of Dutch Beef as long, Tongues a Fortnight; Collard Beef eight or ten Day; Dry them in a Stove, or Wood Chimney, the latter is the best.

A Leg of *Pork Ham* Fashion.

The Pork must be cut like a Ham: then a Quart of ordinary Salt, and a Quart of Bay-salt, and heat it very hot: mix it with a Pound of coarse Sugar, and an Ounce of Salt-petre beaten fine, and rub the Ham well with it, and cover it all over with what is left, for it must go all on, and let it lie three Days, then turn it every Day for a Fortnight then take it out of the Pickle and smoke it as hot as you can.

To Dry *Hams*

Take to every two Ounces of Salt-petre, a Pint of Petre-salt, and rub it well after it is finely beaten over your Ham, and then beat a Pint of Bay-salt and rub over it, and every three Days turn it, it, and when it is laid nine or ten Days hang it in Wood smoak to dry, Do a Hogs Head this Way. To a Ham of Pork or Mutton, have a Quart of Bay-salt, half a Pound of Petre-salt, a quarter of a Pound of brown Sugar all beaten very fine, mix'd together, and rubb'd over it, let it lie a Fortnight; turn it often, and then hang it up one Day to drain, and dry it in Wood smoke.

To Salt Neats Tongues to be dry'd.

Take to every Tongue two Ounces of Salt-petre and beat it very fine, and rub it over the Tongue well, then take a Pint of Petre-salt and rub that over, and every three Days turn it. When it hath laid nine Days in Salt, dry it in the smoke of a Wood Fire. A Hogs Head is salted the same Way as you do the Neats Tongues, and dry'd the same.

Beef dry'd after the Yorkshire Way.

Take the best part of a fat Buttock of a fat Ox, and cut it in what shape you please; then take a Quart of Petre-salt and as much good Bay-salt as will salt it very well, and let it stand in a cold Cellar ten Days in Salt, in which time you must turn it and rub it in the Salt; then take it out of the Brine, and hang it in a Chimney where a Wood Fire is kept for a Month, in which time it will dry and keep a Year. When you eat it boil it tender and when cold cut it in slices, and eat it with Vinegar and Bread and Butter.

To make Mustard.

Chuse good clear Seed and pick it, and wash it in cold Water, drain it, and rub it very dry in a

clean

ean Cloth, then pound it in a Mortar, with the best white Wine Vinegar and ſtrain it, not too thin, and keep it always cloſe cover'd or it will loſe its Strength.

Eggs made to eat like Muſhrooms.

Take ſix Eggs and boil them hard, peel them and cut them in thin ſlices, put a quarter of a Pound of Butter into the Frying-pan and make it hot, then put in your Eggs and fry them quick for half a quarter of an Hour, throw over them a little Salt, Pepper and Nutmeg. For ſauce take a Pint of white Wine, the juice of a Lemon, a Shalot ſhred ſmall, a quarter of a Pound of Butter, and ſtir it altogether, and lay it on ſipets and then ſerve it up.

To make Solomongunda.

Take ſome of the fleſhy part of a Turkey, and the like quantity of a Chicken minced very ſmall, a few hard Eggs and half the whites, ſome Anchovies, Capers and Muſhrooms minced very ſmall, a little Sorrel, Cives and Spinage: Mix and mince all theſe well together, pour over it the juice of Orange, Oil and Vinegar and ſerve it: Garniſh it with Barberries.

To make Sauſages.

Take a Pound of the Fleſh of a leg of Pork and ſhred it fine, then take a Pound of Hog's fat, and cut it ſmall with a Knife, and to every Pound of Fleſh and Fat, take half an Ounce of white Pepper, one large grated Nutmeg, a Pennyworth of beaten Cloves and Mace, a Spoonful of ſhred Sage, and two or three tops of Roſemary cut very fine, and
Salt

Salt it to your Palate, mix all these well together with a little cold Water, and so fill your Guts prepar'd for that purpose.

Sausages of Veal or Lamb.

Take some of the Lean of a Leg of Veal, or Lamb, cut it small and pound it in a Morter, season it with Salt, Pepper, Cloves, Mace and Nutmeg, temper it well together, put in a little Sage chopt, and three or four yolks of Eggs; make them long like Sausages, upon a Pig-plate, then fry them with sweet Butter, turn them often in the Pan, you may roll them in yolks of Eggs before frying.

Veal or Mutton Cutlets.

Dip them in melted Bacon, and season them with all Sorts of savory Herbs, Salt and Pepper, and strew over them the Crumbs of white Bread, broil them over a Stove and serve them up with Gravy instead of Gravy, you may serve them up with a Ragoo of Sweet-breads, Mushrooms and Morels. Garnish with fry'd Parsley and Lemon.

To make Bolonia Sausages.

Take a piece of red Gammon of Bacon and half boil it, and mince with it the same quantity of Bacon Lard, and put to them minc'd Sage, Thyme, Pepper, Salt, Cloves, Mace and Nutmeg finely beaten, the yolks of two or three Eggs to bind it, and as much red Wine as will bring it to a thick Body; mix them well with your Hands, and fill them in large Skins, and hang them in a Chimney (where Wood is burnt) to dry; take care they are not smoked.

To melt Butter, and restore it when Oil'd.

First put your Butter with a little cold Water into a Sauce-pan, dash some Flour out of your Drudger upon it, put it on a slow Fire, shake the Sauce-pan always one Way, do this often, if it turns to Oil, pour about a Spoonful of cold Water in it, and shaking it well in your Hand will recover it.

To clarify Butter.

Melt your Butter in a large glaz'd Pot, on a gentle clear Fire, put a little Water to it and shake them well together, when it is cold, take away the Curds and Whey from the Butter, do this three or four times, the last time put in a Spoonful of Orange-flower Water, and shake it well together, and pour it into your Gallipots for use; stop it down with a Bladder and Leather. This will keep some Time.

Parsley and Butter.

Tye the Parsley together by the shanks, boil it a little, then cut away the shanks and chop the Leaves with a Knife, puting it into your Bason, pour in your melted Butter and stir it about, before you bring it to Table, but if you are to pour it over any Meat, mix it in the Sauce-pan.

Also when you are to have Liver-sauce, boil the Liver, chop and mix it as you do the Parsley, only put it in a little Ketchup, or any Thing proper to relish it.

Caper Sauce; chop your Capers, put them in your Bason, and stir them before they are sent to Table.

To make good Gravy.

Take a Pound of Gravy-beef, a small Onion a bit of Thyme, Parsley, Sweet Marjoram, Pepper and Salt to your Taste, put it in the Stew-pan with some Butter or Water, simmer it a full Hour on the Fire and then strain it through a sieve. It will yield about a Quarter of a Pint.

Directions concerning Garden Things.

To boil Greens.

MOST People spoil Garden Things by over boiling them, all things that are Green should have a little Crispness, for if they are over boil'd they neither have any sweetnels or Beauty.

If you want to have your Greens boil very green put a Handful of Salt among the Water wherein you boil them.

You should boil your Potatoes always on a flow Fire, wich will be a means to prevent their breaking.

Of Soops, Broths and Gravy.

THE best method of boiling Broths is over a Stove, and let it be uncovered, for the cover being on, causes it to boil black.

To make Broth for Soups or Gravy

Chop a Leg of Beef to pieces, set it on the Fire in about four Gallons of Water, scum it very clean season it with white Pepper, a few Cloves, and a bunch of sweet Herbs. Boil it till two thirds is wasted, then season it with Salt; let it boil a little while longer, then strain it off, and keep it for your use.

To make a fine white Soup.

Take a Leg of Beef and a Knuckle of Veal, and let them boil at least four Hours, then beat a Pound of sweet Almonds very fine; and mix them with some of the Broth, then strain off the rest from the Meat, and serve it with the Almonds in it, and sipets of fried Bread.

To make Solid, or Portable Soup.

Get a Leg of Veal, or any other young Meat, cut off all the fat, and make strong Broth after the common Way, put this into a wide Bason, or a Stew-pan well tinned, let it stew gently over a slow Fire till it is boiled away to one third of the Quantity, then take it from the Fire, and set it over Water that is kept constantly boiling, this being an even heat and not apt to burn to the Vessel, in this manner let it evaporate, stirring it often till it becomes (when cold) as hard a substance as Glue, then let it dry by gentle warmth and keep it from moisture.

When you use it, pour boiling Water upon it it makes excellent Broth, either strong or small according to the Quantity you put in. It will keep good at least twelve Months.

To

To make Pease Soup.

Boil a Quart of good feed Pease tender and thick, ſtrain and waſh it through with a Pint of Milk, then put to it a Pint of ſtrong Broth boil'd with Rolls, ſome Spare-mint, and a dry'd French Roll, ſeaſon it with Pepper and Salt, cut a Turnip in Dice, fry it and put in.

Another Way.

Make two Quarts of good Broth from Beef, and pickled Pork; take Cellery, Turnip, Onion, Mint and all Sorts of Kitchen Herbs, ſtew them down tender with a piece of Butter, rub all theſe through a ſive, and one Pint of Peas boiled to a palp, rub them through a ſive, thinning it with your Broth, till all is through. Seaſon it with Pepper and Salt, take ſome Cellery and Leeks cut ſmall to put in the Soup.

White Peas and green Peas are both done this Way. Fry ſome Bread to go in it.

Vermicelly Soup.

Take two Quarts of good Broth made of Veal and Fowl, put to it about half a quarter of a Pound of Vermicelly, a bit of Bacon ſtuck with Cloves, take the bigneſs of half an Egg of Butter and rub together with half a Spoonful of Flour, and diſſolve it in ſome Broth to thicken your Soup, let your garniſh be a Rim on the outſide of it, cut a Lemon ſoke your Bread in your Diſh with ſome of the ſame Broth, take the Fat off, and put your vermicelly in your Diſh, and ſerve it up.

Celery

Celery Soup.

Take some good Gravy and strong Broth, of each the like quantity, take four bunches of Celery, ten Heads of Endive, and wash them, the outside being taken off, cut them in pieces about an Inch long. This Soup may be brown or white; if brown put your Herbs into two Quarts of boiling Gravy, being first blanch'd in boiling Water five or six Minutes, then take the Crust of two French Rolls, and boil them in three Pints of Gravy, strain it through a Strainer, and put it to the Herbs when they are near ready, with a Pullet in the middle, and some bread well soak'd in the Broth.—In all Soups you must not put in your Thickening till your Herbs are very tender.

Onion Soup.

Take two Quarts of strong Veal Broth, fourteen large Onions and cut them thin, and fry them tender, then burn half a quarter of a Pound of Butter Black, and toss up your fry'd Onions, and put them in, then stew them half an Hour in your Broth, and take the Yolks of eight Eggs well beaten six Spoonfuls of Spanish Wine, and put them in a quarter of an Hour before you serve them up, and keep stirring till you send it away. Let your Bread be cut in Dice and fry'd.

Of Gravy Soup.

Cut a Pound of Mutton, a Pound of Veal, and a Pound of Beef into little pieces, put it into seven or eight Quarts of Water, with an old Fowl beat to pieces, an Onion, a Carrot, some white Pepper and Salt, a small bunch of sweet Herbs, two blades of Mace, three or four Cloves, some Celery, Cabbage, Endive, Turnips and Lettuce. Let it stew over a slow Fire till half is wasted, then strain it off for use.

For making a Calves Head Soup.

Stew a Calves Head tender, then strain off the Liquor, and put into it a bunch of sweet Herbs. Onion Mace, some Pearl Barley, Pepper and Salt boil all a small time. Serve up with the Head in the Middle, boned.

Garnish with bread toasted brown, and grated round the rim.

Rice Soup.

Rice Soup you may make as Vermicelley Soup, only your Rice being boiled tender in Water, and it must boil an Hour in strong Broth, and half an Hour will boil Vermicelly.

A good English Soup.

Take a Shin of Beef, a bit of bacon not too salt, and half a pound of Rice, set them on the Fire in as much Water as you think will boil them to rags, keep it cover'd all the while, when the goodness of the Meat is gone strain it off, and put to it some whole Pepper, some Cloves, Mace and Salt, and a Quarter of a Pound of Vermicelly, put in the middle of it a boil'd Fowl, with Spice, some Thyme and Marjoram, and serve it up in a deep soup Dish.

Crack the bone of a Leg of Beef in two or three parts, put it in about a Gallon of Water, then put in two or three blades of Mace, a crust of Bread, Salt,

Salt, and a bunch of Parsley, boil it till the Beef and sinnews are tender, cut some toasted Bread into square pieces and lay in your Dish, lay in your Meat and then pour your Soup over it, and serve it up.

Mutton Broth.

Boil the Scrag-end of a Neck of Mutton, in about four Quarts of Water, then put in an Onion, a bunch of sweet Herbs, and a crust of Bread. Boil it an Hour, then put in the other part of the Neck, after that some dried Marigold, Turnips, Chives, and Parsley chopped small; put these in about ten Minutes before your Broth is enough, Season it with Salt thickened with Oatmeal, others thicken it with Rice, and others Bread, then serve it up.

For making Jelly Broth for Consumptive Persons.

Take a Joint of Mutton, a Capon, a Fillet of Veal, and five Quarts of Water, put these in an Earthen Pot, and boil them over a gentle Fire till one half be consumed, then squeeze all together, and strain the Liquor thro' a Linen Cloth.

A strong Broth.

Take three or four Gallons of Water, and put therein a Leg and Shin of Beef cut into five or six Pieces; boil it twelve Hours, now and then stir it with a stick and cover it close, when it is boil'd, strain and cool it, let it stand till it will Jelly then take the Fat from the Top, and the dross from the bottom.

Fine

Fine Gravy.

Take a lean piece of Beef cut in thin slices well beaten, and fried brown with a lump of Butter, till the goodness is out, put the Meat aside, and put into the Gravy a Quart of strong Broth, half a Pint of Claret, four Anchovies, a Shallot, and some Lemon-peel, Cloves. Mace, Pepper and Salt let all boil together, and when your Gravy is ready, put it into a Gallipot, and set it by till it is call'd for.

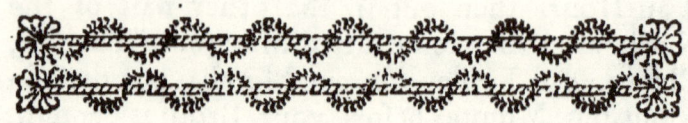

BAKING.

For baking Beef the French Way.

FIRST bone and take away the Skin and Sinnews, then lard it with fat Bacon, season your Beef with Cloves, Salt and Pepper, then tie it up tight with a Pack thread, and put it in an earthen Pan, some whole Pepper, an Onion stuck with ten Cloves, and put at top a bunch of sweet Herbs, two or three Bay leaves, a quarter of a Pound of Butter, and half a Pint of Claret or white Wine Vinegar, cover it close, bake it four or five Hours; serve it hot with it's own Liquor, or you may serve it cold in slices, to be eat with Butter and Vinegar.

To bake Beef like red Deer.

Take a Pound of Beef and slice it thin, and half a Pint of white Wine Vinegar, some Cloves and

Mace about an Ounce, three Nutmegs, pound them altogether, Pepper and Salt, according to your difcretion, a little Sugar. mix thefe together, take a Pound and a half of Suet, fhred and beat it fmall in a Mortar, then lay a row of Suet, a row of Beef, ftrow your Spices between every lane; then your Vinegar, fo do till you have laid in all, then make it up, but firft beat it clofe with a rowling Pin, then prefs it a Day before you put it into your Pafte.

For baking a Calves Head.

Firft wafh it clean, then halve it, and beat the yolks of three Eggs and rub it over with a Feather on the outfide, then take fome grated Bread, fome Pepper, Salt, and Nutmeg, Lemon-peel grated with fome Sage cut fmall; then ftrew this mixture, over the outfide of the Head with fome bits of Butter, put fome Water in the Difh and bake it in a quick Oven, when done, pour over it fome ftrong Gravy with the Brains firft boiled and mixed in it. Garnifh it with Lemon.

For baking of Herrings.

Put fifty Herrings into a Pan, cover them with two parts Water, and one part Vinegar with a good deal of All-fpice, fome Cloves, a bunch of fweet Herbs, a few Bay-leaves and two large Onions, tie them down clofe and bake them, when they come out of the Oven, heat a Pint of red Wine hot and put to them, then tie them down again, and let them ftand four or five Days before you open them, and they will be very fine and firm.

For

For making Ginger Bread.

Take half a Pound of brown Sugar, a Pound and a half of Treacle, two Eggs beaten, one Ounce of Ginger beaten and sifted, of Mace, Cloves and Nutmeg all together half an Ounce beaten very fine, Coriander-Seeds, and Carraway-Seeds of each half an Ounce; two Pounds of **Butter melted** mix all these together, with as much flour as will knead it into a pretty stiff Paste; then roll it out and cut it into what form you please, then bake it in a quick Oven on Tin-plates; a little Time will bake it.

Directions for making PIES *and* PASTES.

Puff Paste.

LAY down a Pound of Flour, break into it two Ounces of Butter and two Eggs, then make it into a Paste with cold Water, work a Pound of Butter to the stiffness of your Paste; and roll out your Paste into a square Sheet, stick it all over with bits of Butter, roll it up like a Collar, then double it up at both Ends, that they may meet in the middle, roll it over again as aforesaid, and then use it.

Paste for High-Pies

Lay down a Peck of Flour, work it up with three Pounds of Butter, melted in a Sauce-pan of boiling Liquor, make it into a stiff Paste.

A

A Lear for Pasties.

Season your Bones of that Meat you put into your Pastie, cover them with Water and bake them, when they are bak'd, strain the Liquor into the Parsley.

For making Minced Pies

Parboil about a Pound of tender lean Beef, add to it a Pound of fine Suet, two fine large Pippins, a quarter of a Pound of Raisins of the Sun stoned, chop them all small together, and sweeten it with Lisbon Sugar, then put in a Pound of Currants well pick'd and dry'd, some All-spice, a little Salt, Lemon-peel, some Angelica and candid Orange-peel, mix them all well together, and moisten with some Sack or Brandy which you like best, and it may be kept a Month, if you chuse to lay any part of it by.

For making a savory Chicken Pie.

Season six small Chickens with Mace, Pepper and Salt, both inside and out, then take three or four Veal Sweetbreads seasoned with the same, and lay round them a few forced Meat-balls, put in some Water and Butter and bake it, then take white Gravy not very strong, and shred a few Oysters and some Lemon-peel, squeeze in some Lemon Juice, not to make it too sour; if you have no Oysters take the whitest of your Sweetbreads, boil them, cut them small and put them in your Gravy thicken it with Butter and Flour, when you open the Pie, if there is any fat skim it off, and pour the above sauce over the Chickens Breasts, so serve it up without any Lid.

A

A Pigeon Pie.

Truſs and ſeaſon your Pigeons with Pepper, Salt and Nutmeg, lard them with Bacon, and ſtuff them with forc'd Meats, lay on Lamb-ſtones, Sweetbreads, and Butter, and cloſe the Pie, pour in Liquor made of Claret, Gravy, Oyſter-liquor, two Anchovies, a Fagget of ſweet Herbs, and an Onion; boil this up, and thicken it with brown Butter. This Liquor ſerves for ſeveral Sorts of Meat and Fowl Pies.

How to make a Turkey Pie.

Bone your Turkey and ſeaſon it with Savory and Spice, lay it in the Pie, and two Capons cut into pieces, in order to fill up the corners. A Gooſe Pie may be made in the very ſame Manner, with two or three young Rabbits to fill up the Corners.

For making a Gooſe Pie

Make the Walls of a Gooſe Pie that your Cruſt be juſt big enough to hold the Gooſe, firſt have a pickled dried Tongue, boiled tender enough to peel, cut off the Root, bone the Gooſe, and a large Fowl; take half a quarter of an Ounce of Mace beat fine, three Tea-ſpoonfuls of Salt, a Tea-ſpoonful of beaten Pepper, and mix altogether; ſeaſon both Fowl and Gooſe with it, then put the Fowl into the Gooſe, and the Tongue into the Fowl, and lay the Gooſe in the ſame form as if whole: Put half a Pound of Butter on the top, and lay on the Lid. This Pie is excellent either hot or cold, and may be kept a great while; a ſlice of this Pie makes a pretty ſide Diſh for Supper.

Another

Another Way

Parboil your Goose, then bone it and season it with Pepper and Salt, and put it into a deep Crust with Butter both under and over it, let it be well baked. then fill it up at the vent hole with melted Butter. Serve it up with Mustard, Bay-leaves, and Sugar.

For making a Green Goose Pie.

Take two fat green Geese, bone them, then season them high with Pepper, Salt, Nutmeg and Cloves, and you may if you like it add a couple of whole Onions in the seasoning. lay them one on another and fill the sides, then cover them with Butter and bake them.

How to make a young Rook Pie.

Cut young Rooks, flea and parboil them and put a Crust at the bottom of your Dish with some Butter and forc'd Meat Balls, then season the Rooks with Salt, Pepper, Mace, Cloves, Nutmeg, and some sweet Herbs, and put them in your Dish, pour in some of the Liquor they are parboiled in and lid it, when baked, cut it open and skim off the Fat, warm and pour in the remainder of the Liquor they were parboiled in, if you think your Pie wants it.

A good common Crust for large Pies.

Take half a Peck of Flour, the Yolks of two small Eggs, boil some Water and put in half a Pound of dried Suet, to which add near a Pound of Butter. Take off the Suet and Butter, and use as much of the Liquor as will make it into a light Crust

Crust, it must be worked well; and roll'd out as usual.

A standing Crust for large Pies of any Sort.

Take half a Peck of Flour, Butter three Pounds, boil the Butter in two quarts of Water, scum it off, and add it to the Flour, but take care to take as little of the Liquor as possible, work it into Paste, pul it in pieces till cold, and it is ready for the use you design it.

A good Crust with cold Water.

To every pound of Flour, rub in half a Pound of Butter, and the Yolk of a small Egg, in the making use cold Water.

A good Crust with Beef Dripping.

To every Pound of Flour, half a Pound of Beef Dripping; mannage your Dripping thus, it must be boiled in cold Water, then take off the Fat and strain it; let it stand till cold, then scrape it and boil it three or four times over, then work it as fine as you can, and make it into a Paste with cold Water.

For making a Giblet Pie.

First scald then pick your Giblets and set 'em on the Fire with Water enough to cover them, season them very high with Pepper and Salt, an Onion and a bunch of sweet Herbs. When they are stewed very tender, take them out of the Liquor and let them stand to cool, afterwards put them into a standing Pie, or into a Pan with some good Puff-paste round it, a proper quantity of Butter, and the Yolks of hard Eggs, forced Meat Balls may be laid over them, leaving a Hole on the top of the Lid, to pour in half of the Liquor which the Giblets were stewed in, just before your Pie is set in the Oven, if there is any Occasion, the remainder of the Liquor heated hot when it is cut open.

For making a Venison Pasty.

First bone a Haunch or Side of Venison, then cut it square, and season it with Salt and Pepper; make it up in your Paste, a Peck of Flour for a Buck Pasty, and three quarters for a Doe; two Pounds of Beef-suet at the bottom of your Buck Pasty, and a Pound and a half for a Doe. A Lamb Pasty is season'd in the same manner as a Doe.

Beef Pasty.

Cut your Beef, and season it over Night with Pepper, Salt and some red Wine and Cochineal and make it up as the Buck Pasty. To each of these pour in a Lear.

How to make a Hare Pie.

Cut the Hare to pieces, then break the Bones and lay them in the Pie, lay on sliced Lemon, force Meat balls and Butter, close it with the Yolks of hard Eggs.

How to make a Rabbit Pie.

First cut your Rabbits in pieces, and fry them in Lard with some flour, season them with Salt, Pepper, Nutmeg, sweet Herbs adding some Broth, when they are cold, lay them in your Pie, adding Morels, Troffels and pounded Lard, lay on the Lid, set it in the Oven, and let it stand for an Hour and a half, when it is about half baked, pour in the Sauce in which the Rabbits were fried, and just

before

before you serve it up to Table, squeeze in some Sevile Orange.

For making Another.

Par-boil a couple of Rabbits. bone, lard and season them with Pepper, Salt, Nutmeg. Cloves, Mace and some Winter Savory, put them in your Pie, with a good many force Meat balls, laying a pound of Butter on the Top, close it up, bake it and when it is cold fill it up with clarified butter.

A Lamb Stone, or Sweet Bread Pie.

Boil, blanch, slice and season them with Pepper, Salt, Nutmeg and Mace; lay them in the Pie with sliced Artichoke bottoms, butter and close the Pie, pour in a Lear.

For making a savory Lamb Pie.

First season the Lamb with Pepper, Salt, Cloves Mace and Nutmeg, then put it into your Crust, with a few sweet-breads and Lamb-stones, seasoned as young Lamb also some large Oysters, and savory force Meat balls, hard Yolks of Eggs, and pour in a little thin Gravy, then put Butter all over the Pie, and Lid it, and set it in a quick Oven an Hour and a half, then make a Lear with Oyster Liquor, as much Gravy, and some Claret, with one Anchovy in it, and a grated Nutmeg; Let these have a boil, thicken it with the Yolks of two or three Eggs, and when the Pie is drawn, put it in.

For making a Mutton Pie.

Pepper and Salt your Mutton Steaks, fill the Pie and lay on Butter, pour in some thin Gravy and close

close it. When it is baked skin the Fat of the Pie, toss up a handful of chopped Capers, Oysters and Cucumbers in Gravy, an Anchovy and drawn Butter and pour them in.

How to make a Pork Pie.

Skin your Pork first then cut into Steaks, and season it well with Salt, Nutmeg sliced, and beaten Pepper, put in some Pippins cut in small pieces as many as you think convenient, and sweeten with Sugar to your Palate, put in half a pint of white Wine, lay Butter all over it, close it up and set it in the Oven.

A Pork Pie for eating cold.

Bone your Loin of pork, and cut part of it into Collops, take also as many Collops of Veal the same size, and beat them both with the back of a Cleaver, season the pork with Salt, pepper, minced Sage, and the Yolks of hard Eggs, season your Veal with Cloves, Mace, Nutmeg, Thyme minced, and the Yolks of hard Eggs, then lay in your Dish a layer of Veal and a layer of pork, till you have laid all your Meat in, then close up your pie, and Liquor it with Safron Water and the Yolks of Eggs. When it is baked and cold, fill it with clarifi'd Butter; remember to let your first and last layer be pork. When baked set by for Use.

Veal Pie to be eat cold.

Raise a high round pie, then cut a fillet of Veal into four or five fillets, and season it with pepper, Salt, Nutmeg, Mace and Cloves, some minced Sage and sweet Herbs and lay it in the pie, with slices

slices of Bacon at the bottom, and between each place lay on Butter and close the Pie. When it is baked and half cold, fill it up with clarifi'd Butters.

The best Ingredients for Sweet Pies.

The Meat, Fish or Fowls, Bolls, Spice, Lemon, Citron, Skirrits, Currants, Raisons, Gooseberries, Damsons, Grapes and Orange-peel candied, Spanish potatoes and a Caudle.

The Ingredients for Savory Pies.

The Meat, Fowls or Fish, savory Spices, shiver'd palates, Cock's Combs and Stones, Lamb-stones, Bacon, Oysters, Mushrooms, Artichoke-bottoms, Truffels and a Lear.

To make Puff Paste for Pies.

Take half a pound of Butter to a Quarter of a Peck of Flour, add some Salt, and then make it into a Paste with some cold Water, then roll it out and stick small pieces of Butter over it, strewing some Flour under it, and roll it over nine or ten different Times, till a Pound or upwards of Butter be rolled in. This is a good Crust for all sorts of Pies.

To make Paste Royal.

Take a Pound and a Half of Flour, a Pound of Butter, an Egg and a quarter of a Pound of fine Sugar bruised fine with a Rolling-pin, work these into a Paste.

Paste for a Pasty.

Knead up a Peck of fine Flour with six Pounds of Butter and four Eggs, with cold Water.

To make a Crust for a raised Pie.

Boil six Pounds of Butter in a Gallon of Water, skim it off very clean, and put it directly into a Peck of Flour, work it well into the Paste, then pull it in pieces till it is cold, and make it up in what Form you chuse.

This will do for a Goose Pie.

A fine Paste for Patty Pans.

Work up a Pound of Flour, with half a Pound of good Butter, two Ounces of fine Sugar and Eggs.

How to make an Apple Pie.

First scald about a dozen large Apples very tender, then take off the Skin and the Core from them and put to it twelve Eggs, but six Whites, beat them very well and take the Crumb of a Penny-loaf grated, and a grated Nutmeg, Sugar it to your Taste, and put a Quarter of a Pound of Butter melted, mix all these together and bake them in a Dish, butter your Dish, and take care that your Oven is not two hot

To make very good Whigs

Take a Quarter of a Peck of fine Flour, and put into it three Quarters of a Pound of fresh Butter, till it is like grated Bread, something more than a Pound of Sugar, half a Nutmeg, some Ginger grated, three Eggs beaten very well, put to them half a Pint of Ale Yeast, make a Hole in your Flour and put in your Eggs, and as much Milk just warm as will make it into a light Paste, let it stand before the Fire to raise half an Hour, then make it into a dozen and a half of Whigs

wash

wash them over with Eggs juſt as you are going to put them in the Oven, and half an Hour will bake them.

How to make an Artichoke Pie.

Take twelve Artichoke bottoms and boil them tender, boil alſo the Yolks of twelve Eggs hard, then take three Ounces of candied Orange, Lemon and Citron-peel, half a pound of Raiſins ſtoned, ſome grated Nutmeg, a blade of Mace, a quarter of a Pound of Sugar, then put theſe into your Pie, with half a Pound of Butter, obſerving to lay the Sweetmeats uppermoſt, when it comes out of the Oven, then put in half a pint of Cream and as much Sack.

For making a Potatoe Pie.

Firſt make your Cruſt, then put in a layer of Butter in the bottom, then boil your Potatoes tender, put them in, and lay upon them Marrow, Yolks of hard Eggs, Orange, Lemon, and blanched Almonds, whole Spice, Dates, Piſtacho's, and Citron-peel candied, then put a layer of Butter over all, cloſe up your Pie and bake it, when it comes out of the Oven cut up the Lid, and pour in melted Butter, Wine, Sugar, and three Yolks of Eggs.

How to make a Herring Pie.

Take ſome pickled Herrings, ſoak them well in freſh Water, take off their ſkins whole, mince your Fleſh with two Roes, put ſome grated Crumbs of Bread, ſeven or eight Dates, Roſe Water, ſome Sack with Safron and Sugar, make of theſe a good ſtiff Paſte, then fill your Skins with this Farce.

lay

lay Butter in the bottom of your Dish, lay in your Herrings and Dates with them, and on the Top of them lay Goofeberries, Currants and Butter, then clofe it, bake it, and when done Liquor it with Vinegar Butter and Sugar,

For making an Eal Pie.

Skin and clean your Eals, feafon them with fome Nutmeg, Pepper and Salt, cut them in long pieces, you muft make your Pie with good Butter pafte, let it be oval with a thin Cruft, lay in your Eals length ways, putting over them fome frefh Butter, then bake them.

To make an Oyfter Pie.

Firft par-boil a Quart of large Oyfters in their own Liquor, then mince them fmall, and pound them in a Mortar with Marrow, piftacho Nuts, and fweet Herbs, one Onion and favory Spice, and a fmall Quantity of grated Bread, or feafon them in the fame Manner whole, lay on Butter and clofe the pie.

To make a Trout Pie.

Clean and fcale your Trouts, and lard them with pieces of a filver Eal rolled up in Spice, and fweet Herbs, and Bay-leaves powdered, lay between and on them the Bottoms of fliced Artichokes Oyfters, Mufhrooms, Capers and fliced Lemon, lay on Butter and clofe the pie.

To make a Tench Pie.

Make your Cruft, then put on a layer of Butter, fcatter in grated Nutmeg, Cinnamon and Mace, then put in fix Tench, lay over them more Butter, Spice and a few new Currants, pour in a
Quarter

Quarter of a pint of Claret, and let the Pie be baked well, when it comes out of the Oven put in melted Butter, and dust it over with fine Sugar, and serve it up.

Of TARTS.

To Ice Tarts.

TAKE a Yolk of an Egg, and melted Butter, beat it very well together, and with a Feather wash over your Tarts and sift Sugar on them just as you put them in the Oven.

A short Paste for Tarts.

Rub a Pound of Wheat Flour and three quarters of a Pound of Butter together, put three spoonfuls of Loaf Sugar to it, beat and sifted, the Yolks of four Eggs beat very well. put to them a spoonful or two of Rose Water, and work them all together into a Paste, then roll them thin and ice them over, and bake them in a slow Oven.

To make a Gooseberry Tart.

Take your Crust, then sheet the bottoms of the Patty-pans, and strew them over with powder Sugar, then take green Gooseberries and fill your Tarts with them, and lay a layer of Gooseberries and a layer of Sugar, so close your Tarts and bake them in a quick Oven, and they will be very fine and Green.

To make a Cherry Tart.

Take two Pound of Cherries, bruise, stone and stamp them, and boil up their juice with Sugar; then stone four Pounds more of Cherries, and put them into the Tart with the Cherry Syrup, bake your Tart and serve it up.

To make black Tart stuff.

To a dozen Pound of Pruens, take half a dozen of Maliga Raisins, wash and pick them clean, and put them into a Pot with Water, set them over the Fire till all these are like Pulp, and stir them often least they burn too, then take them off, and let them be rubbed thro' a Hair Sive hard with your Hands till all is through, then season them to your taste with fearced Ginger.

To make yellow Tart stuff.

Take 24 Eggs and beat them with Salt together, and put into it a Quart of seething Milk, stirring it till it crudles then take it off, and put it into a Napkin, hanging it up till all the Whey is run through, when it is cold take and grind it in a Stone Mortar with Sack and Sugar to your taste, and otherwise to make it look white, leave the Yolks, and in stead of Sack put Rose Water.

A proper Paste for Tarts.

Take three quarters of a Pound of Butter mixed well with a Pound of Flour. Or thus, Take equal Quantities of Flour, Butter and Sugar mixed well together, then beat it with a Rolling-pin and roll it thin.

The best Rules to be observed in making PUDDINGS.

FOR boiling Puddings, always take care the Bag or Cloth be very clean, and dip'd in hot Water and then well Floured. If a batter Pudding tie it close, if a Bread Padding tie it loose, and be sure the Water boils before pou yut the Puddings in, and you should move the Puddings in the Pot after, for fear they should stick. When you make a batter Pudding, first mix the Flour well with Milk, then put in the Ingredients by degrees, and it will be free from lumps, but for a plain Batter Pudding, the best way is to strain it through a coarse Hair Sive, that it may neither have lumps nor the treads of the Eggs, and in all other Puddings strain the Eggs when they are beat. If you boil them in Bowls or China Dishes, butter the inside before you put in the Batter, and for all baked Puddings, butter the Pan or Dish before the Pudding is put in.

For making a very fine Pudding.

Take a Pint of boil'd Cream, put into it some Nutmeg and Mace; then take the Crumb of two french Rolls and put them into the boiled Cream, then take the Yolks of six Eggs, and about twenty almonds beat very small, half a Pound of Marrow, mingle these well together and season it with some Sugar and Salt, and send it to the Oven.

A very good Plumb Pudding, and not expensive.

Take a Quart of Milk, twelve Ounces of Currants, the like quantity of Raisins of the Sun stoned, a Pound and a half of Suet choped small, eight Eggs, and four Whites, half a Nutmeg grated, some beaten Ginger, a spoonful of Brandy, a few sweet meats, and mix'd up very stiff with fine Flour. You may bake it or boil it. Take care the Oven be not over hot.

For making a boiled Plumb Pudding.

Shred a Pound of Beef-suet very fine, and add three quarters of a Pound of Raisins stoned, then take some grated Nutmeg, a large spoonful of Sugar and some Salt, four Eggs, some Sack, three spoonfuls of Cream, and six spoonfuls of Flour, mix these well together, tie it up in a Cloth and let it boil three Hours, pour melted Butter over it.

For making a Bread Pudding.

Put a quarter of a Pound of Butter to a Pint of Cream, set it on the Fire and keep it stirring, the Butter being melted, put in as much grated Bread as will make it very light, some grated Nutmeg and Sugar, three or four Eggs and some Salt, mix all these well together, butter a Dish, put it in and bake it half an Hour.

For making an Apple Pudding.

Scald six or eight Codlings, take out the Cores, and cut them into pieces, put some Cinnamon and Sugar, roll them into a fine Paste tied up in a clean Cloth, about an Hour will boil it, then pour into it some melted Butter and Cream, and serve it up.

For making a light Pudding.

Put some Cinnamon, Mace and Nutmeg into a Pint of Cream, and boil it; when it is boiled take out the Spice, then take the Yolks of eight Eggs, and four of the Whites, beat them well with some Sack, then mix them with your Cream, some Salt and Sugar, take a Half-penny white Loaf, and a spoonful of Flour, some Rose Water, beat all these well together, and wet a thick Cloth and flour it, then put your Pudding into it and tie it up, and when the Pot boils it must boil an Hour. Melt Butter and Sugar and pour over it.

To make Almond Pudding.

Take a Pound of Almonds blanched, beat them very small with some Rose Water, boil good Milk with a slice of Mace, and some sliced Nutmeg, when it is boiled take it clean from the Spice, then take the Quantity of a Penny-loaf and grate it, scarce it thro' a Cullendar, then put it into the Milk and let it stand till it be cold, then put in the Almonds and five or six Yolks of Eggs, some Salt and Sugar, what you think fit and good store of Beef-suet, and Marrow very finely shred.

For making a cheap, baked Rice Pudding.

Take a quarter of a Pound of Rice, boil it in a Quart of Milk, stir it that it does not burn, when it begins to thick take it off, let it stand till it is almost cold, then stir in well a quarter of a Pound of Butter, and Sugar to your Palate; grate a small Nutmeg, butter your Dish, pour it in, and bake it.

For

For making a Rice Pudding.

Take half a pound of ground Rice, set it on the Fire with three Pints of new Milk, boil it well, and when it is almost cold, put to it eight Eggs well beaten, and put half the Whites, with half a Pound of Butter, and half a Pound of Sugar, put in some Nutmeg or Mace. It will take about half an Hour to bake it.

For making a Batter Pudding.

Take six Eggs and a Pint of Milk, and four spoonfulls of Flour, put in some Salt and half a grated Nutmeg, you must take care your Pudding is not too thick, flour your Cloth well. Three quarters of an Hour will boil it. Serve it with Butter, Sugar and some Sack.

For making a Quaking Pudding.

Beat eight Eggs very well, put in them three spoonfuls of Wheat Flour, a Pint and a half of Cream, some Salt, boil it with a stick of Cinnamon, a blade of Mace, when it is cold mix it, butter your Cloth, do not give it over much room in the Cloth. About an Hour will boil it, you must turn it in the boiling, or the Flour will settle, serve it up with some melted Butter.

To make a Pudding to bake.

Take a Penny Loaf and pare it, slice it in a Quart of Cream with some Rose Water, and break it very small, take three Ounces of Jordan Almonds blanched and beat small with some Sugar, put in eight Eggs beaten, a Marrow-bone, and three Pippins sliced thin or any way, mingle these together and put in some Ambergrease if you please.

For

For making a Potatoe Pudding.

Boil four large Potatoes as you would for eating, beat them with some Rose Water and a glass of Sack in a Marble Mortar, put to them half a Pound of Melted Butter, half a Pound of Currants well clean'd, some shred Lemon-peel and candied Orange, mix all these well together, bake it and serve it up.

For making a Gooseberry Pudding.

Pick, coddle, bruise and rub a quart of green Gooseberries, through a Hair Sive to take out the Pulp, take six spoonfuls of the Pulp six Eggs, half a Pound of clarified Butter, three quarters of a Pound of Sugar, some Lemon-peel shred fine, a handful of Bread-crumbs or biscuit, a spoonful of Rose Water or Orange-flower Water, mix these well together and bake it with Paste round the Dish, you may if you please add Sweetmeats,

For making an excellent Black Pudding.

Take a quart of Hog's Blood, a quart of Cream, ten Eggs beaten well together, stir them well and thicken it with Oatmeal finely beaten and grated Bread, Beef-suet finely shred, and Marrow in little lumps, season it with some Nutmeg, Cloves and Mace mixed with Salt, some sweet Marjoram, Lemon, Penny-royal and Thyme, shred very well together and mixed with others, when all is well mixed, fill the Guts, being well cleansed, and boil them carefully.

A good boiling Pudding.

Take a pound and a quarter of Beef-suet, after it is skin'd shred it very fine, then stone three quarters of a Pound of Raisins, and mix with it a little Salt, four Eggs and four spoonfuls of Cream, and about half a Pound of fine Flour, mix these well together pretty stiff. tie it in a Cloth, and let it boil four Hours. melt Butter thick for sauce.

A good baking Pudding.

Take a Pound of Beef suet, shred it as small as for minc'd Pies, a Pound of Flour, a Pound of Currants, a quart of Milk. a Penny Loaf, you must boil your bread in your Milk, and when it is cold mix the other things with it, and six Eggs, some Nutmeg, Sugar and Salt to your taste, It will take two Hours baking.

A Plumb Pudding without Suet.

Take a Pint of Milk, mix it with Flour very thick, six Eggs, four of the Whites left out, half a Pound of Currants, half a Pound of Raisins of the Sun stoned. some Nutmeg and beaten Ginger, two spoonfuls of Brandy, half a spoonful of Rose Water, half a Pound of melted Butter, mix it well and boil it two Hours.

To make a boiled Pudding.

Take a Pint of Cream or Milk, boil it with a stick of Cinnamon a little while, and take it off, and let it stand till it be cold, put in six Eggs, take out three Whites, beat your Eggs before you put them into the Milk, then stir them together, and take a Penny-roal and slice it very thin, let it lie and soak, and break it very small, then put in some Sugar, and butter the Cloth before you put it in. it will take but a little Time seething, and when you take it up, melt some fresh Butter and some
Sack

Sack and Sugar, beat all these together and put it into the Dish with your Pudding to be served in.

To make white Puddings.

After the Humbles be very well boiled, take some of the Lights with the Hearts, and all the Flesh and Fat about them, pricking from them all the Sinnews and Skins, then chop the Meat as small as can be, then put to it some of the Liver very finely searsed, some grated Bread searsed, four or five Yolks of Eggs, a Pint of Cream, a spoonful or two of Sack, a little Sugar, Cinnamon, Cloves and Mace some Nutmeg, a few Carraway-seeds, a little Rosewater, mingled with a good deal of Swine's Fat, some Salt, roll it in rolls two Hours before you go about it, let the fat side of the Skin be turned and steaped in Rose-water till you fill them.

For making Marrow Puddings.

First boil a pint of Cream, and the Marrow of two Bones, except a few bits to lay on the Top, then slice a Penny white loaf in it; when it is cold, put into it half a Pound of blanched Almonds, beaten fine, with two spoonfuls of Rose-water, the Yolks of six Eggs, a glass of Sack, a little Salt, six Ounces of candied Citron and Lemon sliced thin, mix altogether, then lay the bits of Marrow, bake and serve it; you may add half a Pound of Currants.

☞ When you boil Cream take care to stir it all the Time.

For making a Custard Pudding.

Beat five or six Eggs in a Pint of Cream, with two spoonfuls of Flour, half a Nutmeg grated some

Salt and Sugar to your Taste, butter a Cloth, and put it in when the Pot boils, boil it exactly half an Hour, and melt Butter for Sauce.

CAKES, CHEESE-CAKES, CUSTARDS.

Of Cakes.

How to make a Pound Cake.

TAKE a Pound of Butter, beat it in an earthen Pan with your Hand one Way, till it is like a thin Cream; then have ready twelve Eggs, but six Whites, and beat them up with the Butter, a Pound of Flour beat in it, a Pound of Sugar and a few Carraways; beat it all well together for about an Hour with your Hand or a great Wooden Spoon; butter a pan and put it in, then bake it a Hour in a quick Oven.

Some like a Pound of Currants in it.

How to make a Plumb Cake.

Take three Pound of Flour, the like weight of Currants, one Pound of Sugar, one Pound of Butter, the like weight of Orange and Lemon-peel candied, and set on all with Milk, luke-warm, a little Nutmeg, Allspice, Ginger, Cloves and Mace, half a Pint of Yeast and four Eggs.

Another Way.

Take half a Peck of Flour, half a Pint of Rosewater, a Pint of Cream, a Pint of Ale Yeast, boil it, then add a pound and a half of Butter, six Eggs without

without the Whites, four Pounds of Currants, half a Pound of Sugar, one Nutmeg and a little Salt, work it very well and let it stand an Hour by the Fire, then work it again and make it up, and let it stand an Hour and a Half in the Oven. Take care that the Oven be not two hot.

Shrewsbury Cakes.

Take a Pound of Sugar, three Pound of fine Flour, a Nutmeg grated, some beaten Cinnamon, the Sugar and Spice must be sifted into the Flour, and wet with three Eggs, and as much melted Butter as will make it of a good thickness to roll into a Paste, mould it well and roll it, cut it into what shape you please, perfume them and prick them before they are put into the Oven.

To make a good Seed Cake.

Take two Pounds of Butter beaten to a Cream, a Quarter of a peck of Flour, a Pound and three Quarters of fine Sugar, three Ounces of candied Orange peel and Citron, one Ounce of Carraway seeds, ten Eggs and but five Whites, a little Rosewater, a few Cloves, Mace and Nutmeg, some new Yeast and half a Pint of Cream, then bake it in a Hoop, and butter your Paper, when it's baked, ice it over with the Whites of Eggs and Sugar, and set it in again to harden.

How to make a light Seed Cake.

Take half a Quartern of Flour, some Nutmeg and Ginger, three Eggs well beat, three spoonfuls of Ale Yeast, half a Pound of Butter, and six Ounces of smooth Carraway seeds, and work it warm with your Hand.

To make a good Seed Cake.

Take six Pounds of fine Flour, rub into it a Thimble full of Carraway feeds finely beaten, and two Nutmegs and Mace finely beaten; then heat a Quart of Cream hot enough to melt a Pound of Butter in it, and when it is no more than blood warm, mix your Cream and Butter with a Pint of good Ale Yeast, and then wet your Flour with it, make it pretty thin; just before it goes into the Oven, put in a pound of rough Carraway-feeds, and some Citron sliced thin, three quarters of an Hour in a quick Oven will bake it.

For making a cheap Seed Cake.

Put a Pound and a half of Butter in a Sauce-pan, with a pint of new Milk, set it on the Fire, take a pound of Sugar, half an Ounce of All-spice beat fine, and mix them with a Peck of Flour. When the Butter is melted, pour the Butter and Milk in the middle of the Flour and work it up like Paste, pour in the Milk, half a pint of good Ale Yeast, and set it before the Fire to raise, just before it goes into the Oven. You may either put in some Carraway seeds or Currants and bake it in a quick Oven.

If you make it in two Cakes, they will take an Hour and a half baking.

For making Mackeroones.

Take a Pound of Almonds, let them be scalded, blanched and thrown into cold Water, then dry them with a Cloth, and pound them in a Mortar, moisten them with Orange-flower Water, or the White of an Egg, least they turn to Oyl, after-wards

wards take an equal Qantity of fine powder'd Sugar, with three or four Whites of Eggs and a little Musk, beat all well together, and shape them on Water-paper with a spoon round. Bake them in a gentle Oven on Tin.

To make Curd Cakes.

Take a pint of Curds, four Eggs, take two of the Whites, put in some Sugar, a little Nutmeg and a little Flour, stir them well together, and drop them in, and fry them with a little Butter.

Of CHEESE-CAKES.

For making Cheese-Cakes.

TAKE the Curd of a Gallon of Milk, three quarters of a Pound of fresh Butter, two grated Biscuits, two Ounces of blanched Almonds pounded with a little Orange-flower Water, half a Pound of Currants, seven Eggs, Spice and Sugar, beat it up with some Cream till it is very light, then fill your Cheese-cakes.

Another Way.

For the Crust take half a pint of Flour, and four spoonfuls of cold Water, and three parts of a quarter of a Pound of Butter, beat and knead these together, and put the Paste asunder several times, then roll it square, and turn it over, then take a Pint of Cream and seven Eggs, and a quarter of a Pound of Sugar, and a quarter of a Pound of Currants plump before you put them in, and a whole
Nutmeg

Nutmeg grated on a Knife, and some Pepper beaten but not too much, it muſt be gently boiled and ſtirred as you do butter'd Eggs, the ſtuff muſt be cold; and then put it in the Coffin and ſo bake it.

For making Rice Cheeſe-Cakes.

Boil two Quarts of Cream or Milk a little while, with ſome whole Mace and Cinnamon, then take it off the Fire, take out the ſpice and put it on the Fire again, and make it boil, ſtirring it together, then take it off, and beat the Yolks of twenty-four Eggs, ſet it on the Fire again, and keep it continually ſtirring till it is as thick as Curds; add half a Pound of blanched Almonds pounded, and ſweeten it to your Palate. Or, if you chuſe it, you may put in half a Pound of Currants, well picked and rubbed in a clean Cloth.

A good Cheeſe-Cake.

Take two Quarts of Milk or Cream, and the Yolks of eight Eggs, and but four Whites, beat them very well and ſet it on the Fire, when it boils take it off and ſtrain the Whey gently from it, to the Curd, put ſome Nutmeg grated and ſome Cinnamon beat, four ſpoonfuls of Roſe-water, and as much Sack, a Quarter of a Pound of Currants, ſome Butter and fine Sugar, and grated Naples Biſcuits: You may put to it what Cruſt you pleaſe.

For making Lemon Cheeſe-Cakes.

Take two large Lemon peels, boil and pound them well together in a Mortar, with about ſix Ounces of Loaf Sugar, the Yolks of ſix Eggs, and half a pound of freſh Butter; pound and mix,

all

all well together, and fill the Patty-pans about half full.

Orange Cheese-Cakes you may do the same way, but be very careful to boil the peel in two or three Waters, to take out the bitterness.

Of CUSTARDS.

A proper Crust for Custards.

A Pound of Flour, requires three Quarters of a pound of Butter, the Yolks of four Eggs, a few spoonfuls of Cream, mix all well together, and let it stand ten or twelve Minutes, then work it and roll it very thin.

For making a Custard.

Boil a Quart of Cream or Milk, with a stick of Cinnamon, large Mace and a quartered Nutmeg, when half cold mix it with eight Yolks of Eggs, and four Whites well beat, some Sack, Sugar and Orange flower Water, set all on the Fire, and stir it till a white froth rises, which skim off, then strain it and fill your Crusts, which should be first dried in the Oven, and which you must prick with a Needle before you dry them, to prevent their rising in blisters. Or you may put it into Cups, without the paste.

Another Custard.

Boil a Quart of Cream, with a blade of Mace; beat ten Eggs, put half the Whites, take the Mace out,

out and when almoſt cold, beat in the Eggs, with one ſpoonful of Orange flower Water; ſweeten it to your taſte, and put it into your Cuſtard-cups, and let them juſt boil up in the Oven, and if you boil the Eggs in the Cream altogether, then you may put it into your Cuſtard-cups over Night, and they will be fit for uſe.

For making a Cream Cuſtard.

Grate the Crumb of a penny Loaf very fine, and mix it with a good piece of Butter, and a Quart of Cream, beat the Yolks of twelve Eggs with Cream, ſweeten them with Sugar, let them thicken over the Fire, make your Cuſtard ſhallow, bake them in a quick Oven, and when they are baked, ſtrew fine Sugar over them.

To make a Gooſeberry Cuſtard.

Take as many Gooſeberries as you pleaſe, boil them till they be ſoft, then take them out, and let them ſtand and cool, then drain them, draw them with your Hand through a Canvas ſtrainer, then put in a little Roſe-water, Sugar and three Whites, and ſtir them altogether, put them in a Skillet, and ſtir them apace, elſe they will burn, let them ſtand and cool a little while, take them off and put them in a glaſs.

For making common Biſcuits.

Beat up ſix Eggs with a ſpoonful of Roſe-water, a ſpoonful of Sack, then add a pound of fine powder'd Sugar, and a pound of Flour, mix them into the Eggs by degrees, and an Ounce of Coriander ſeeds, mix all well together, ſhape them on white thin paper, on Tin Moulds, in any Form you

you please: beat the white of an Egg with a Feather, rub them over, and dust the Sugar over them set them in an Oven moderately heated, till they rise, and come to a good colour, take them out; and when you have done with the Oven, if you have no Stove to dry them in, put them into the Oven again, and let them stand all Night to dry.

To make a White Pot.

Take a pint and a half of Cream, a Quarter of a pound of Sugar, a little Rose Water, a few Dates, and a little large Mace, a sliced Pippin or Lemon cut sippet fashion for the Dishes you bake in, and dip them in Sack or Rose Water.

For making plain Custards.

Take a Quart of new Milk, sweeten it to your taste, grate in some Nutmeg, beat up eight Eggs well, leave out half the Whites, stir them into the Milk, and bake it in China Basons, or put them into a Kettle of boiling Water, taking care that the Water does not come above half way up the Basons, for fear of its going into them. You may add a small glass of Brandy, or some Rose Water in your making.

For making an Almond Custard.

First blanch your Almonds, then pound them in a Mortar very fine, and add a little Milk in the beating, press it through a Sieve, and make it as the Custard above-mentioned, and bake it in Cups.

For making a whip'd Syllabub.

Take a Pint of Canary, two Quarts of Cream, some Whites of Eggs and a Pound of fine Sugar, and

and beat it with a Whisk till it froths well; then take and skim off the Froth, and put it into Syllabub Glasses.

How to make a Gooseberry Fool.

Take your Gooseberries and pick them, and put them into cold Water, and boil them till they be all so thick that you cannot discern what it is, to the Value of a Quart, take the Yolks of six Eggs well beaten with Rose Water, and before you put in your Eggs, season it well with Sugar, then strain your Eggs and let them boil a little while, then take it up and put it in a broad Dish and let it stand till it be cold, thus it must be eaten.

To make Apple Cream at any Time.

Take twelve Pippins, pare and slit them, then put them in a Skillet and some Claret Wine, and a race of Ginger shred thin, a little Lemon-peel cut small, and some Sugar. Let all these stand together till they be soft; then take them off and put them in a Dish till they be cold, then take a quart of Cream, boil it with some Nutmeg a while, then put in as much of the Apple stuff to make it of what thickness you please, and serve it up.

To make Clouted Cream.

Take three Gallons of new Milk, set it on the Fire till it boils, make a Hole in the middle of the skum of the Milk, then take a Bottle or three Pints of very good Cream, put it into the Hole you made in the middle of the Milk as it boileth, and let it boil together half an Hour, then put it in three or four Milk-pans, so let it stand two Days if the Weather be not too hot then take it up in

Clouts

Clouts with a Scummer, or a Slice, and put it in that which you will ferve it in, if you like it feafoned, you may put fome Rofe Water between every Clout as you lay one upon another with a Slice in the Difh you mean to ferve it in.

To make Quince Cream.

Take the Quinces and put them in boiling Water unpared, then let them boil very faft uncovered that they may not colour, and when they are very tender, take them off and peel them, and beat the Palp very fmall with Sugar, and then take raw Cream and mix with it till it be of a fit thicknefs to eat like a Cream, with a ftick of Cinnamon, it muft ftand till it be cold before you put it to the Quinces.

To make a Trifle Cream.

Take fome Cream and boil it with a cut Nutmeg, add Lemon peel a little, then take it off to cool, feafon it with Rofe Water and Sugar to your tafte: Let this be put in the thing you ferve it in then put in fome Runnet to make it come, then it is fit to eat.

To make Angellets.

Take a quart of new Milk and a pint of Cream, put them together with fome Runnet, when it is come well; take it up with a fpoon, and put it into the Vat foftly and let it ftand two Days till it is pretty ftiff, then flip it out and falt it at both ends, and when you think it is falt enough, fet it a drying, and wipe them, and within a Quarter of a Year they will be fit to eat.

To make Bread without Yeast.

To accomplish this, you must procure a Lump of about two Pounds of the Dough of your last making, which had been raised by Yeast; it must be kept in a wooden Vessel, and cover'd with Flour: *This is called Leaven,* The Night before you intend to bake, put the said Lump of Dough into about a Peck of Flour, and work them well with warm Water; it must lie in a Vessel of Wood, cover'd with a Linen Cloth, and a Basket, remember to keep it warm; the next Morning it will rise so as to be sufficient to mix with more than two Bushels of Flour, being worked up with warm Water and some Salt. When sufficiently worked, let it be covered as before, till you find it rise then kneed it well, and make it into what Form you think fittest for baking. the more Leaven is put to the Flour, the better and lighter the Bread will be.

How to make a very good Tansie.

Take sixteen Eggs and six of the Whites, beat them very well, then put in some Sugar and some Sack, beat them again and put about a Pint or some more of Cream, then beat them again, put in the juice of Spinnage or of Primrose leaves to make it green, then put in some more Sugar, if it be not sweet enough beat it again, and so let it stand till you fry it, when the first course is in, then fry it with some sweet Butter, it must be stirred and fryed very tender, when it is fryed enough, then put it in a Dish, strew some Sugar upon it and serve it in.

To make Furmenty.

Take a Quart of sweet Cream, two or three sprigs of Mace and a Nutmeg cut in half, put it into your Cream, so let it boil, then take your French Barley or Rice, being first wash'd clean in fair Water three times and pick'd clean, then boil it in sweet Milk till it be tender, then put it into your Cream and boil it well, and when it hath boiled a good while, take the Yolks of six or seven Eggs, beat them very well, to thicken on a soft Fire, boil it and stir it, or it will quickly burn, when you think it is boiled enough, sweeten it to your taste, or so serve it with Rose Water and Musk Sugar, in the same manner you make it with Wheat.

To make a Sack Posset.

Take two Quarts of pure good Cream, a quarter of a Pound of the best Almonds. stamp them in the Cream and boil Amber and Musk therein, then take a Pint of Sack in a Bason, set it on a chafing Dish till it be Blood warm, then take the Yolks of twelve Eggs, six Whites and beat them very well together, and so put the Eggs into the Sack, make it good and hot, let the Cream cool a little before you put it into the Sack, then stir all together over the Coals till it be as thick as you would have it, if you take some Amber and Musk and grind in it small with Sugar, and strew it on the top of the Posset, it will give it a most delicate and pleasant Taste.

To make Gallendine Sauce for a Turkey.

Take some Claret Wine, some grated Bread, a sprig of Rosemary, some beaten Cloves and beaten Cinnamon, and some Sugar.

To make Leach.

Make your Jelly for your Leach, with Calves Feet, as you do your ordinary Jelly; but a little stiffer, and when it is cold take off the top and bottom, and set it over the Fire with some Cinnamon and Sugar, then take your Turnsels, well steap'd in Sack, and crush it and so strain it in your Leach and let it boil to such a thickness, that when it is cold you may slice it.

To make Cheese Loaves.

Take the Curds of a tender new Milk Cheese, and let them be well pressed from the Whey, and then break them as small as you can possible, then take Crumbs of Manchit and Yolks of Eggs, with half the Whites and some sweet Cream, and some fine Flour, mingle all these together, and make a Paste of it but not too stiff, then make them into small Loaves and bake them, when they be baked cut off the tops, and butter them with Sugar, Nutmeg and melted Butter and put it in with a Spoon, and stir it altogether, then lay on all the tops, and serve them with scraped Sugar.

To make a fresh Cheese.

Take a Pint of fresh Cream, set it on the Fire, then take the Whites of six Eggs, beat them very well, and wring in the Juice of good Lemon to the Whites, when the Cream seeths up, put in the Whites, and stir it about till it be turned and then take

take it off, put it in the Cheese-cloth, and let the Whey be drawn from it, then take the Curd and pound it in a stone Mortar with some Rose Water and Sugar, pound it in an earthen Cullendar, and so let it stand till you send it to the Table, then put it into a Dish, put some sweet Cream to it and so serve it in.

Of JELLIES.

Currant Jelly.

PICK a Gallon of ripe Currants from the Stalks and put them in a Pan, bruise them well with your Hands, then strain off the Juice, and to every Pint take three Quarters of a Pound of fine loaf Sugar, put them in your preserving pan together, and let them boil till they Jelly, which will be in about twenty Minutes, and then pour them into Glasses.

Calves Foot Jelly.

Take four Calves Feet, clean wash'd and bon'd put a Gallon of Water with four Ounces of Hartshorn, boil it to a Jelly, then run it thro' a Bag, and clarify it with six Whites of Eggs, add to it a Quart of white Wine, and the juice of five Lemons, and six Pippins slic'd, sweeten it with the best Sugar to your taste, so boil it up and run it through your Bags into Glasses.

To

To make a Chrystal Jelly.

Take two Calves Feet, slice them and lay them in fair spring Water with a Knuckle of Veal, shift it in half a dozen Waters, take out the Fat betwixt the Claws, but do not break the Bones, for if you do the Marrow of the Bones will stain the Jelly, when they are soft and pick'd very clean, boil them very tender in spring Water, when they be boiled tender take them up, and use them at your pleasure to eat, let the Broth stand in a Pot or Pipkin till it be cold, then take away the bottom and the top, and put the clear into a fair Pipkin, put into it half a Pound of fair Sugar candy or other Sugar, three drops of Oil of Nutmeg, three drops of Oil of Mace, and a grain of Musk; and so let it boil leisurely a quarter of an Hour, then let it run through a Jelly Bag into a Glass Pot, when it is cold you may serve it in litttle careless Lumps being taken out with a Child's spoon, and this is the best way to make your Chrystal Jelly.

Hartshorn Jelly.

Take a Pound of Hartshorn and put it to three Quarts of Spring Water, put it over a slow Fire, and let it boil gently till it comes to a Quart, then strain it off, and let it stand till it is cold then take the gross part off, and put to it the juice of four Lemons and Sugar to your Taste, and the Whites of four Eggs, boil all these up gently, and run them thro' your Bag into your Glasses,

☞ In all the Receipts for making Jellies, you must observe, that after your Jelly has passed thro'
the

the ag Bonce, you muſt put it in the ſecond time by little and little and ſo on, till you find your Jelly does not fall fine readily, you muſt take the ſhells of your Eggs and break them ſmall, and boil them up in your Jelly, and ſo run it through your Bag.

To make Jelly of Pippins or Codlins.

Take ſix Pippins or Codlins, pare and ſlice them into a Quart of Spring Water, boil it till it comes to a Pint, ſtrain it and put to the clear a Pound of fine Sugar, boil it till it will Jelly, ſcum it clean as it boils; this Jelly is proper to put a little on the top of any red or white preſerves.

Of CANDYING.

To Candy Cherries.

GET them before they are full ripe, ſtone them and having boiled your fine Sugar to a height, pour it on them, gently moving them, and ſo let them ſtand till almoſt cold, and then take them out and dry them before the Fire.

To Candy all Kind of Flowers, in way of Spaniſh Candy.

Take double refined Sugar, put it into a Poſnet with as much Roſe Water as will melt it, and put into it the Pap of a roaſted Apple, and a grain

R   of

of Musk, then let it boil till it comes to a Candy height, then put in your Flowers, being pick'd, and so let it boil; then cast them on a fine Plate, and cut it in Wafers with your Knife, then you may spot it with Gold and keep it.

To Candy all Kind of Fruitage, as Oranges, Lemons, Citrons, Lettice-stocks, &c.

Take one Pound of refined Sugar, put it into a Posnet, with as much Water as will wet it, and so boil it till it comes to a Candy height, then take all your Fruit being preserved and dried, then draw them through your hot Sugar, then lay them on your Hurdle, and in one Quarter of an Hour they will be finely candied.

To Candy Barberries and Grapes.

Take preserved Barberries, wash off the Syrup in Water, and sift fine Sugar on them, then let them be dry'd in the Stove, turning them from time to time, till they are thorough dry. Preserved Grapes may also be candy'd after the same manner.

To Candy Orange or Lemon Peel.

Having steep'd your Orange-peels as often as you shall judge convenient in Water, to take away the bitterness; then let them be gently dry'd and candy'd with Syrup made of Sugar,

To Candy Apricots.

You must slit them on one side of the Stone, and put fine Sugar on them; then lay them one by one in a Dish, and bake them in a pretty hot Oven; then take them out of the Dish and dry them on Glass Plates in an Oven for three or four Days.

Preserving *and* Confectionary.

To preserve Cherries in Liquid.

TAKE the best Morello Cherries when ripe, either Stone them or clip their Stalks off, and to every Pound take a Pound of Sugar, and boil it till it boils strong, then put in the Cherries, and by degrees bring them to boil as fast as you can, that the Sugar may come all over them, scum them and set them by, the next Day boil some more Sugar to the same Degree, and put some Jelly of Currants, drawn as hereafter directed; *For Example.* If you boil the Pound of Sugar, take one Pint of Jelly, put in the Cherries and the Syrup to the Sugar; scum them and fill your Glasses or Pots, take care as you cool to disperse them equally, or otherwise, they will swim all to the top.

To draw Jelly of Currants.

Wash your Currants, put them into a Pan and mash them; then put in some Water and boil them to a Pomish, then strew it on a Sieve and press out all the Juice, of which you make the Jelly for all the wet Sweet-meats that are red.

To Preserve green Grapes.

Take the largest and best Grapes before they are thorough ripe, stone and scald them, but let them lie two Days in the Water they were scalded in, then drain them and put them into a thin Syrup, and give them a heat over a slow Fire, the next Day turn the Grapes in the Pan and warm them again, the Day after drain them and put them into clarified Sugar, give them a good boil and scum them, set them by; the next Day give them another good boil, scum them and set them in a warm Stove all Night, the Day following drain and lay them out to dry, first dusting them very well.

To preserve Currants.

Part them in the tops, lay a lane of Currants and a lane of Sugar, and so boil them as you do Rasberries, do not put in the Spoon but scum them, boil them till the Syrup be thick, then take them off, and let them stand till they be cold, and put them into a Glass.

To preserve Damsons.

Take as many as you please, and weigh as much Sugar as they weigh, and strew some on the bottom, and some on the top, and you may wet the Sugar with some Syrup of Damsons and a little Water, then set them on the Fire, and let them stand and soak softly about an Hour, then take them off and let them stand a Day or two, then boil them till you think they be enough, take them off, and put them up.

To

To preserve Grapes.

Stamp and strain them; let it settle a while before you wet a Pound of Sugar or Grapes with the Juice, stone the Grapes, save the Liquor, in the stoning take off the Stalks, give them a boiling, take them off and put them by.

To preserve Rasberries.

Take as many Rasberries as you think fit, stamp and strain the Juice from them, then take either white Currants or Gooseberries boiled in Water, as you do when you preserve Currants, and take as much of the white Liquor as you have Juice of Rasberries, and mix them together, then take the weight of it in Sugar, and set it on the Fire, and boil it very fast, till it be almost ready to Jelly, then as it boils put in the whole Rasberries, and continue boiling it till they are clear and tender, then take out the Rasberries and lay them into Glasses, if the Jelly be not enough, boil it a little more, then strain it out into the Glasses.

To preserve Pippins.

Take a Pint and a half of the smallest white Wine, and three Pounds of fine Sugar, dissolve the Sugar with the Wine and Water, and clarify it with the Whites of two new lay'd Eggs, by running it through a Jelly Bag, to this thus clarified put two Pounds of Kentish Pippins without Fault, being finely pared, then put them in the Sugar as aforesaid; then let them boil so fast that you cannot see any Pippins, till they be near boiled, which you may

may know by the conftant taking them in a Spoon all the while they boil; fcum them dilligently, and a little before they are boiled enough, fqueeze in the Juice of two good Lemons: Let the Time you preferve them be about May-day old Stile.

To preferve white or red Currants.

Take the largeft Currants you can get, pull them off the Stalks and ftone them, put a Pint of Currants to a little more than a Pint and a half of Water, fet them on a quick Fire and boil them very faft, till the goodnefs of the Currants be almoft boiled out, then ftrain it gently through a Bolter, and to the Liquor, take the weight of Sugar, melt the Sugar in the Liquor, then put in your ftoned Currants, and boil them very faft, till they are clear and tender, then take them off, and lay the Currants in their Glaffes, ftrain the Jelly through a Bolter and fill the Glaffes, if it will not Jelly by that Time the Currants be out, give it one boil after: Do red the fame way, only make the Liquor you boil it in of white Currants.

To preferve Walnuts.

Gather the Walnuts about Midfummer, or 14 Days after, and put them into Spring Water, then put them into a Kettle of boiling Water, and let them boil half a quarter of an Hour, then fhift them into another Kettle, and do fo three or four Times, then drain them well, and lard them with Citron: to every Pound of Nuts, put one Pound

of

of Sugar, make that into a Syrup and clarify it, then put the Nuts into it, and let them lie in the Syrup twenty-four Hours, then boil them in the Syrup half an Hour, then put them into a Pan and let them stand till next Day, then boil them an Hour more, so put them up for Use.

To preserve Damsons, or black Plumbs.

Take their weight in Sugar, and enough of Water to cover them; so boil them a little, being close covered, and turning them that they may not spot, suffer the Plumbs to boil no faster than the Syrup keeps under them, when they are boiled take them up, and boil the Syrup till it be thick, then put your Plumbs and it together in Glasses, the Damsons should be split.

To preserve Currants.

Take red or white Currants, the best and largest Bunches, before they be too ripe, tie three or four Bunches together, then take the weight of them in fine Sugar, dissolve the Sugar in a little spring Water; boil it and scum it clean, then put in the Fruit, and boil them gently five Minutes: Let them cool; boil them as long; do so three times: Then take the Fruit, and put them into Pots or Glasses. Boil the Syrup till it will drop a Pearl, without breaking. Put a white Paper over your Pots or Glasses, and tie a Parchment over that.

Preserve Rasberries the same way, but boil them gently.

To preserve Barberries.

Take them ripe and of a good colour, and the Sort without Stones, then take three times the weight of them in fine Sugar, boil some of the worst Barberries in spring Water, strain it and take as much of it as will dissolve the Sugar. Boil it to a Syrup, scum it clean, tie the Fruit in Bunches, and do them as the Currants.

To preserve Rasberries.

Take as many as you please, a lay of Sugar and a lay of Rasberries, and so lay them in a Skillet, and as much Water as you think will make Syrup enough and boil them, and put two Spoonfuls of Water in, scum it, take it off and let it stand.

To preserve Fruit green all the Year.

Gather your Fruit, when they are three parts ripe, on a very dry Day, when the Sun shines on them, then take earthen Pots and put them in, cover them with Corks, or bung them that no Air can get into them, dig a Place in the Earth a Yard deep, set the Pots therein, and cover them with the Earth very close, and keep them for Use. When you take any out, cover them up again as at first.

To pickle Walnuts.

Make a Pickle of Salt and Water, strong enough to bear an Egg, boil and scum it well, and pour it over your Walnuts, let them stand twelve Days, changing the Pickle at the end of six Days, then pour them into a Cullendar, and dry them with a

coarse

coarse Cloth, then get the best white Wine-Vinegar, with Cloves, Mace, Nutmeg, Jamaica Pepper-corns, sliced Ginger, boil up these and pour it scalding hot upon your Walnuts, you may add some Shallot and a Clove or two of Garlic, to one hundred of Walnuts, you must put a Pint of Mustard-seed, when they are cold, put them into a Jarr and stop them close.

To preserve Walnuts whole.

Take the largest French Walnuts, when full grown, before they are hard, pare off the green to the white, and put them into clean Water, then throw them into boiling Water, and boil them till very tender, then drain them and put them in clarified Sugar, giving them a gentle heat the next Day, scum them and put them by, then drain and put them on Plates, dust them and put them in a Stove to dry.

To preserve Walnuts black.

Take the smaller Sort of Walnuts when full grown and not shell'd, boil them in Water till very tender, but not to break, so they will become black, then drain them and stick a Clove in every one, put them into your preserving Pan, and if you have Peach-Syrup or that of white Walnuts, it will do as well or better than Sugar, put as much Syrup as will cover the Walnuts, boil them very well, then scum them and set them by, the next Day boil the Syrup a little, then put in the Walnuts, and give them a good boil, the next Day after drain them

them and boil the Syrup very well, adding more Syrup if occafion, give all a boil, fcum them and put them into your Pots for Ufe.———Note, *Thefe Walnuts are never offer'd as a Sweet-meat, being of no Ufe but to purge gently the Body, and to keep it open.*

To preferve green Plumbs.

Take green Plumbs grown to their full bignefs, but before they begin to ripen, let them be carefully gather'd with the Stalks and Leaves, put them into cold fpring Water over a Fire, and let them ftand over a gentle Fire till they are foft, put two Pounds of double refined Sugar to every Pound of Plumbs, and make the Sugar with fome Water into a thick Syrup, before the Pumbs are put in; the Stones of the Plumbs are not to be grown hard but that you may thru a Pin through them, After the fame way do Apricots.

To put Plumbs in Jelly.

Any Sort of Plumbs are agreeable in Jelly, and the fame Method will do for all as for one. When your Plumbs are preferved in their Sugar, and you have drain'd them in order to put them in a fecond, they are then fit to put to Liquor, which you muft thus: Drain the Plumbs and ftrain the Syrup through a Bag, then make a Jelly of fome ripe Plumbs and Codlins together, by boiling them in juft as much Water as will cover them, prefs out the Juice and ftrain it, and to every Pint of Juice boil one Pound of Sugar very ftrong, put in the

the Juice and boil it a little; then put in the Syrup and Plumbs, and give them a good boil, then let them settle, fcum them and fill your Glaſſes or Pots.

To dry Plumbs. Pears, Apples. Grapes &c.

First preſerve them and then wipe them, and ſet them on Tin-plates over a Stove or in a ſlack Oven, and turn them very often. Obſerve always that your Fruit have their Stalks on.

To preſerve white ripe Grapes.

Take the Grapes and ſtone them, and to a Pound of Grapes put a Pound of double refined Sugar, dip the Sugar in Water, ſet it over the Fire and let it boil to a Candy height, and have a Skillet of boiling Water, and then put your Grapes into it, then put them in the Sugar and boil them a little, dip them into the hot Water as faſt as you can. ſo let them boil pretty faſt till they look clear; then put them into your Glaſſes with the Jelly. If you dry any of them, lay them on Plates and dry them in the Sun.

To preſerve Gooſeberries.

Take what Quantity of Gooſeberries you pleaſe, ſlit them on the ſides, and pick the Stones out with a Needle, and put them into cold Water, ſet them on the Fire and ſcald them gently, then let them ſtand in the Water they are ſcalded in, till they are almoſt cold, then peel the Skin off and lay them in double refin'd Sugar, then take the Weight

S 2 of

of them in Sugar, which wet in the Water your Gooseberries were scalded in, and boil them in Water till they are slippy, before you boil them fast, that they loose not their Colour.

To make Wafers.

Take a Pint of Flour, a little Cream, the Yolks of two Eggs, a little Rose-water, with some searched Cinnamon and Sugar, work them together, and bake upon hot Irons.

To make Conserve for Tarts all the Year.

Take Damsons or other good ripe Plumbs, and peel off the Skins and so put them in a Pott to Pippins pared, and cut in Pieces, and so bake them, then strain them through a Piece of Canvas, and season them with Cinnamon, Sugar, Ginger and a little Rose-water, boil it upon a Chafing Dish of Coals, till it be as thick as a Conserve, and then put it into your Gally-pots, and you may keep it good all the Year.

To keep Quinces all the Year.

First you must core them, and take out the Kernels clean, keep the Cores and Kernels and set over some Water to boil them, then put them in the Water and let them boil till they be soft, then take them up and set them down till they be cold, then take the Kernels and stamp them, and put them into the same Water they were boiled in, and let them boil till they be thick, see you have as much Liquor as will cover the Quinces; and if you have

not

not enough, take of the smallest Quinces and stamp them, to make more Liquor, and when it is boiled good and thick, you must strain it thro' a coarse Cloth, and when the Quinces be cold, then put them into a Pot, and the Liquor also, and be sure the Liquor covers them, you must lay some Weight upon them to keep them under, so cover them close and let them stand 18 Days, and they will work of their own accord, and they will have a thick Rind upon them, and when they grow heavy or thick, then take it from the Liquor, for it will have a Skin on it within a Month or six Weeks.

PICKLING and PRESERVING.

Rules to be observed in Pickling.

NEVER Use any Thing but Stone Jars for all Sorts of Pickles that require hot Pickle to them, for Vinegar and Salt will penetrate thro' all Sorts of Earthen Vessels. Stone and Glass are the only Thing to keep Pickles in. Be sure never put your Hands to take Pickle out, it will soon spoil them. The best way is to every Pot tie a Wooden Spoon, full of small Holes, to take the Pickle out with. Let your Brass Pans for green Pickles, be exceeding bright and clean, otherwise your Pickles will have no Colour; use the very Best and Strongest white Wine Vinegar, likewise be very exact in watching when your Pickles begin to boil, and change

change Colour, so that you may take them off the Fire immediately, otherwise they will loose their Colour, and grow soft in keeping. Cover your Pickling Jars with a wet Bladder and Leather.

To pickle Cucumbers.

Take the Cucumbers and wash them clean, dry them in a Cloth, then take some Water, Vinegar, Salt, Fennel-tops, and some Dill-tops, and some Mace, make it fast enough, and sharp enough to the Taste, then boil it a while, and then take it off, let it stand and be cold, then put in the Cucumbers, and lay a Board on the top to keep them down, and tie them close, and within a Week they will be fit to eat.

Another way.

Make a strong Pickle of Salt and Water, so as to bear an Egg, and boil it, pour it boiling hot upon the Cucumbers, and let them stand two Hours, then take Vinegar with some Pepper and Mace; then put your Cucumbers in it, set it on the Fire, hang your Pot pretty high, and let it simmer till they look Green, but do not let it boil, then take them off and cover them close; the next Day boil your Pickle and pour it over them again.

To pickle large Cucumbers in slices.

Get large Cucumbers before they be too ripe, slice them the thickness of Crown Pieces, in a Pewter Dish: To every Dozen of Cucumbers, slice two large Onions thin, and so on till you have filled
your

your Dish with a Handful of Salt between every Row, then cover them with another Pewter Dish, and let them stand 24 Hours, then put them in a Cullendar and let them drain very well, put them into a Jar, cover them with white Wine Vinegar, and let them stand four Hours, pour the Vinegar from 'em into a Copper Saucepan, and boil it with some Salt, put to the Cucumbers some Mace, whole Pepper, a large race of Ginger sliced, and then pour the boiling Vinegar on, cover them close, and when they are cold, tie them down. They will be fit to eat in two or three Days.

To pickle small Cucumbers.

Take them fresh gather'd, put them in a Pan, and pour on them as much hot boiling Brine as will cover them. Let them stand close cover'd 24 Hours, then take them out and dry them, and put them into the Pot you intend to keep them in, with Cloves, Mace, Pepper, some Dill and Fennel, a little Horse-raddish, some Lemon-peel, and a few Bay-leaves, pour on them as much boiling hot Vinegar as will cover them. Do thus three times in three Weeks, keep them close stop'd and hot six Hours a Time, and if they be not Green, make your Vinegar boil, and put in the Cucumbers, and let them boil up six Minutes.

To pickle Oysters.

Take your Oysters and pick them out of the Shells and save the Liquor that comes from them, then take your Oysters one by one, and wash them clean

out

out of Grist, then strain the Liquor, and take a Quantity of white Wine, and a large Mace or two, and two or three slices of Nutmeg and Pepper, grosly beaten, and Salt them, boil it together, then put in your Oysters and boil them, then take the Yolk of an Egg and beat it well with Wine Vinegar, then take up your Oysters and let them cool, then put in your Egg and let it boil, then take it off, let it cool, and put it together.

Another way.

Take a Bushel of large Oysters, save the Liquor and if that is not enough, add to it some white Wine, half an Ounce of Mace, and as much whole Pepper, let them boil together till you think they are enough, then take out the Oysters, take a quarter of a Pint of Vinegar and white Wine, a Handful of Salt, put it to the Liquor and boil it a quarter of an Hour, put them into an Earthen Pan, and when cold put the Liquor to them.

To pickle Mellons, or large Cucumbers.

Take the largest and greenest Cucumbers, cut out a Piece the length of your Cucumbers, in one of the sides, cleanse the Seeds and dry them well, then pour into them some Cloves, Mace, whole Pepper and bruised Mustard-seed, peel two or three Cloves of Garlic, and the same Quantity of Shallot, some Ginger sliced thin, according to the Quantity you make, and put some Salt, lay the Piece in its Place, that you cut out of the Side, and tie it close with Packthread, and lay them in an

Earthen

earthen Pan, and then put to them as much white Wine Vinegar as will cover them, with half a Pint of made Mustard to three Pints of Vinegar, and a Bay-leaf, with Salt according as you like, let them lie in this pickle nine Days, then put them into a Brass Kettle and set them over the Fire to make them Green, stop them down very close, and let them have one or two boils at a Time, then take them off, let them still be close stop'd and let them stand to green, then set them on the Fire again, and so order them till they are very Green; then take them out of the Pickle, and put them into a Jar or Pot boil the Pickle and put it to them boiling hot, tie them with leather and use them when you please.

To Pickle French Beans.

Take French Beans before they have any strings and lay them in an earthen Pot, and betwixt every lay of Beans a Handful of Salt, then let them stand till they are shrunk, and the Salt pretty well disolved, then cover them with Vinegar. Before you boil them for Use, you must steep them an Hour in Water, then hang them on the Fire, putting them in when the Water is cold, when they are boiled let them stand till they are cold, and cover them with white Wine Vinegar.

Another way.

Take them young before they have any strings, lay them in cold Brine six Days, one Day in fresh Water, then dry them, put them in a Pot with

T whole

whole Spice, Pepper, some Ginger, Lemon-peel, and a few Bay-leaves, cover them with hot boiling Vinegar, and do them as you would small Cucumbers.

To Pickle Mushrooms.

Take the fresh gather'd, (the bottoms are the best) cut the stalks half off, put them in Water and a little Salt; let them lay two Hours, then rub the tops with a piece of Flannel, and as you rub them, put them in clean Water with some Salt; let them lie two Hours, make your Water and Salt boil, then put in your Mushrooms; let them boil eight Minutes, then take them out from the boiling Liquor, and put them hot in cold Water and some Salt, let them lie twenty-four Hours; then dry them and put them into a Glass with some whole Mace, sliced Nutmeg, some Bay-leaves, then boil as much white Wine and Vinegar as will cover them, when it is cold fill up your Glasses and put some sweet Oil on the Top, and tie a Bladder over them.

Another way.

Scoope or peel them, throw them into Water and Salt, skin and strain them tho' a Sieve, put to them Salt and Water made strong, let them lie there three Hours, then put them into Beer Vinegar, let them stand two Days, and put them into white Wine Vinegar, with some Mace, Cloves, Nutmeg, white Pepper and Ginger, boil the Pickle but not the Spice, and let it be cold before you put it to the Mushrooms.

Catchup

Catchup of Mushrooms.

Take a Stew-pan full of large flat Mushrooms, and the tips of those you wipe from Pickling; set it on a slow Fire with a handful of Salt without Water, they will make a great deal of Liquor, which you must strain, and put to it a quarter of a Pound of Shallots, some Pepper, Ginger, Cloves, Mace, and a Bay-leaf, boil and skim it well; when 'tis quite cold, bottle and stop it close.

To Pickle Lettice.

Take Cabbage Lettice, cut off the loose Leaves and the bottom of the Stalks, then cut the Cabbage part and wash them well, boil them in clean Water till they are soft, then lay them on a Sieve to drain for twenty-four Hours, then crush them with your Hands to get the Water out, so lay them close in an earthen Pot, between every row strew some Salt, white Pepper, Ginger sliced, some whole Mace, a clove of Garlick on the Top, fill the Pot with white Wine Vinegar, and put a Paper close to them, and if they mould put a fresh one, as the Vinegar sinks, fill the Pot with fresh, tie them very close, and set them in a close Place.

To Pickle Walnuts.

Take Walnuts very young, not shell'd at all, pare them very thin, scald them well with Salt and Water, and put them into it, give them two or three warms on the Fire, then make ready some more strong Pickle of Vinegar and some Salt, Pepper and Ginger to your taste, then take them out of the Water they was first boiled, put them into the Pickle, keep them close cover'd, after a Month change the Pickle, and thus you may keep them all the Year.

To Pickle Walnuts white.

Pare them till they look white, and put them into Salt and Water as you pare them, then boil them in Salt and Water in a Cloth, but let your Salt and Water boil before you put them in, when they are cold put them in Pickle of raw Vinegar, Pepper, Mace and Nutmeg.

To Pickle small Onions.

Peel your Onions and throw them into Water, then put them into a well tin'd Sauce-pan with Salt and Water, just let them simmer and strain them off, let them stand till they are cold and well drained, then make a Pickle of white Wine Vinegar, the palest you can get, with Mace, sliced Ginger, white Pepper-Corns, and Salt to your taste, give it one boil up, and let it stand till it is quite cold, then add to it about two spoonfuls of the best pale Flour of Mustard, and after you have put your Onions into Jars, pour your Pickle upon them.

Or lay your small hard Onions in Water and Salt and let the Pickle be Vinegar and Spice.

To Pickle a red Cabbage.

Take a red Cabbage and slice it round as thin as possible, boil your Vinegar with Pepper, Salt and Mace, pour it boiling hot on the Cabbage,

and

and stop it down close, let your Pot stand just within the warmth of the Fire for some Time. This is a Pickle of little Use, but for the garnishing of Dishes, Sallads and Pickles, tho' some People are fond of it.

Another way.

Cut off the Stalks and outside Leaves, shred it into thin slices, make a Pickle of Salt, Vinegar, Cloves, Mace, Ginger, and sliced Nutmeg, then boil it, and when it is cold, pour it over the Cabbage, and it will be fit for Use in twelve Hours.

☞ You may do white Cabbage in the same Pickle, only it must be poured on boiling hot two or three Times.

To Pickle Cauli-Flowers.

Take the whitest and closest Cauli-Flowers before they are brown, cut them the length of your Finger from the Stalks, boil them a very little in a Cloth, in Milk and Water, not till they are tender, then take them out and let them stand till they be cold. For the Pickle, take the best white Wine Vinegar, Cloves, Mace, a Nutmeg Quartered, a Bay-leaf, and some Pepper, so let these boil; and when cold, then put in your Cauli-Flowers. In three or four Days they will be fit to Eat.

To Pickle Asparagus to keep the whole Year.

Break the Heads off and put them up in white Wine Vinegar, and Salt to your discretion, so that they

they will be cover'd, then take them out, and boil the Pickle, and scum it very well; if there be Occasion, renew it with Vinegar and Salt, and when they are cold, put them in again, and they will keep a whole Year, use them when you think proper, only boil them tender, and eat them with Butter.

To Pickle Samphire.

Gather your Samphire in May, pick it and lay it for two Days in Salt and Water, then take it out and put it into a Pot, and soak it over a clear gentle Fire, cover it close till it is Green and Crisp, and put it into Pots or Glasses, tie it down close with Bladder or Leather.

To Pickle Beet-roots and Turnips.

Make your Pickle of Water and Salt, Vinegar and some Cochineal, and boil the Beet-roots in it, pare your Turnips, and boil them but half as long as the Roots, then keep them both in this Pickle.

To Pickle Barberries.

Take them ripe and fresh gather'd; put them into a Pot you intend to keep them in. Boil Water and Salt together, but not so strong as to bear an Egg, and when it is cold fill up your Pot.

To Pickle Grapes or Barberries.

Put your Grapes or Barberries in a Pot, then boil Verjuice with a good quantity of Salt, and let it it ſtand till it is cold, and then put in the Grapes or Barberries; and cover them.

For Pickling Currants.

Take Currants either red or white, before they are thorough ripe; you muſt not take them from the Stalk; make a Pickle of Salt and Water, ſome Vinegar, ſo keep them for Uſe.

For preſerving Cherries, with the Leaves and Stalks green.

Take morel Cherries, dip the Stalks and Leaves in the beſt Vinegar boiling hot, ſtick the Sprig upright in a Sieve till they are dry, in the mean time boil ſome double refin'd Sugar to a Syrup, and dip the Cherries Leaves and Stalks in the Syrup, and juſt let them ſcald, lay them on a ſieve, boil the Sugar to a candy height, then dip the Cherries, Stalks Leaves and all, then ſtick the Branches in Sieves, and dry them as you do other Sweetmeats. They look very pretty at Candle-light in a Deſert.

For Pickling Gooſeberries, or Grapes.

Take a quart of white Wine Vinegar, and half a Pint of Water, and as much Sugar as will make it ſweet, boil it for ſome Time, then put them up and cover them cloſe, they muſt not be ripe at all.

For Pickling Currants for preſent Uſe.

Take either red or white Currants, being not thorough ripe; give them a warm in Vinegar, with as much Sugar as will indefferently sweeten them; keep them well cover'd with Vinegar.

For Pickling Pigeons.

Boil them with whole Spice in three Pints of Water, and a Pint of Vinegar, when boiled enough, take them up, and when they are cold keep them in this Pickle.

To Pickle Tongues.

First boil them in Water and Salt, then blanch them, and put them into a Pot: and make the Pickle of as much white Wine Vinegar as will fill it, and boil it up with a faggot of sweet Herbs; when cold put in the Tongues with sliced Lemon, cover it close. When you eat them beat up some of the Pickle with good Oil, and garnish with sliced Lemon.

To Pickle Pork.

Take the principal Pieces of the Pork and Salt them lightly with ordinary Salt, then lay them hollow that the Blood may drain from it, with the fleshy side downwards; let it lie two or three Days amongst the Salt; put some beaten white Pepper and a few Cloves, bruised, salt it well and pack it very close in the thing you keep it in, with the Rind downward, cover it with Salt, and when it has stood three Weeks, put in as much salt Pickle as will cover it, then lay the false bottom on the top to keep it under Pickle, put the ordinary and bony pieces by themselves.

To pickle Herrings or Mackerel.

Take the Fish and cut off the Heads and Tails, gut them and wash them, dry them well, then take two Ounces and a half of Salt-petre, three Quarters of an Ounce of Jamaica Pepper, and a Quarter of an Ounce of sweet Marjoram and Thyme chop'd small, mix them together, and put them within and without the Fish, lay them in an Earthen Pan, the Roots at top, cover them with White Wine Vinegar, then set them in an Oven not too hot, for two Hours. This for Fifteen, and after this Rule do as many as you please.

To pickle Salmon.

Take two Quarts of good Vinegar, Half an Ounce of Jamaica Pepper, Cloves and Mace of each a Quarter of an Ounce, near a Pound of Salt, bruise the Spice grosly, and put all these to a small Quantity of Water, put just enough to cover your Fish, cut your Fish round in three or four Pieces, according to the size of the Salmon, and when the Liquor boils up in your Fish, boil it well, then take the Fish out of the Pickle, and let it cool, when it is cold, put your Fish into the Barrel or Stein you intend to keep it in, strewing some Spicie and Bay-leaves between every piece of Fish, let the Pickle cool, then scum off the Fat, and when the Pickle is quite cold, pour it on your Fish, and cover it very close

To pickle Lobsters.

Boil your Lobsters in Salt and Water, till they will easily slip out of the Shell; take the Tails out whole, just crack the Claws and take 'em out as whole as possible, then make the Pickle half white Wine and half Water, put in whole Cloves, whole Pepper, whole Mace, two or three Bay-leaves; then put in the Lobsters, and let them have a boil or two in the Pickle; then take them out and set them by to be cold, boil the Pickle longer, when both are cold put them together and keep them for Use. Tie the Pot down close, eat them with Oil, Vinegar and Lemon.

To pickle Tench.

When your Tench is cleans'd, have a Pickle ready boil'd, half white Wine and half Vinegar; a few blades of Mace, some sliced Ginger, whole Pepper and Bay-leaf, with a Piece of Lemon-peel and some Salt, so boil your Tench in it, and when it is enough, lay them out to cool, and when the Liquor is cold put them in; it will keep but a few Days.

To pickle Muscles, or Cockles.

Take your fresh Muscles, or Cockles; wash them very clean, and put them in a Pot over the Fire till they open, then take them out of their Shells and pick them clean, then lay them to cool, put their Liquor to some Vinegar, whole Pepper, Ginger sliced thin and Mace, set it over the Fire, when it is scalded hot, put in your Muscles, let them stew a little n little, then pour out the Pickle from them, when both are cold, put them in an earthen Jug, and cork it up close: In two or three Days they will be fit to eat.

To pickle Smelts to exceed Anchovies.

First wash and gut them clean, then lay them in Rows, and put between every layer of Fish, Pepper, Nutmeg, Mace, Cloves and Salt, well mix'd, and four Bay-leaves, powder'd Cochineal and Petre-salt, beat and mix'd with Spice, boil red Wine Vinegar enough to cover them, and put to them when quite cold.

To pickle Purslain.

Take the Purslain and pick it in small Pieces, put it into a Pot or Barrel, then take some Water, Vinegar and Salt to your Taste, it must be very strong of the Vinegar and Salt, put some Mace and boil all these together, and pour this Liquor in seething hot into the Purslain, when it is cold, tie it close, but lay a Piece of Board on the Top to keep it down, and within a Week or two it is fit for Use.

To make Verjuice.

Get the clearest and best Crabs when they are near ripe, lay them in Heaps together, to sweat: Then throw away the rotten Ones, pick out the Stalks and beat them in a Mash, squeeze the Juice thro' a Hair Sieve, put it into Bottles and cork them close.

To distill Verjuice for Pickles.

Take three Quarts of the sharpest Verjuice, and put it into a cold Still, and distill it off very softly, the sooner it is distill'd in the Spring, the better for Use.

An excellent Way to make Vinegar, by which a Person lately acquired a good Fortune.

Put a Pound of coarse Sugar to every Gallon of Water, let it boil and keep scumming it as long as any Scum will arise, it must afterwards be put into Tubs to cool like Beer; when it is cold to work as Beer, toast a large Piece of Bread and rub it all over with Yeast, put this into the Liquor and let it work near thirty Hours, then put the Liquor into a stout Iron-bound painted Cask, which must be set in the Sun, and in such a Place as it can remain in. If made in March it will be fit to use in July: it is best to draw it off into Bottles and keep it for Use. This is the strongest of Vinegar, it will do very well for Pickling, with a third part of cold spring Water to it and be full sour enough, and will likewise when used alone keep most Sorts of Pickles without boiling, nor indeed do I ever use it hot, unless with my green Pickles.

Of Made Wines,

Cowslip Wine.

TO six Gallons of Water put thirty Pounds of Maligo Raisin; boil your Water full two Hours, and measure it out of your Copper upon the Raisins, which must be chop'd small and put in a Tub, let them work together ten Days, stirring it several Times a Day, at the End of that Time strain it off and press the Raisins hard to get out their Strength, then take two spoonfuls of good Ale Yeast and beat with it six Ounces of Syrup of Lemons, then put in three Pecks of Couslips, by little and little, and let all your Ingredients work together three Days, stirring it three or four Times a Day, then tun it up, bottle it at four Month's End.

To make Mead.

To five Quarts of Honey, put sixty Quarts of Water, eighteen Races of sliced Ginger, and one handfull of Rosemary; let them boil three Hours, and be scummed perpetually, when it is cold put Yeast to it, and it will be fit to bottle in eight or ten Days.

Birch Wine, as made in Sussex.

Take the Sap of Birch fresh drawn, boil it as long as any Scum arises; to every Gallon of Liquor

quor put two Pounds of good Sugar, boil it Half an Hour and fcum it very Clean, when it is almoſt cold, fet it with fome Yeaſt fpread on a Toaſt, and let it ſtand five or fix Days in an open Veſſel, ſtirring it often; then take fuch a Caſk as the Liquor will fill, and fire a large Match dipt in Brimſtone, and put it into the Caſk, and ſtop in the Smoke till the Match is extinguiſhed, and as quick as poſſible pour in a Pint of Sack, or Rheniſh, which Taſte you like beſt, for the Liquor retains it; rince the Caſk well with this and pour it out, then pour in your Wine and ſtop it cloſe for fix Months, then if it is perfectly fine you may bottle it.

Sage Wine.

To 24 Pounds of Maligo Raiſins pick'd and ſhred, and fix Gallons of Spring Water well boiled, let it be as cool as Milk from the Cow before you pour it on the Raiſins, then put in half a Buſhel of red Sage groſly ſhred, ſtir all together, and let it ſtand fix Days, ſtirring it well every Day, and cover it as cloſe as you can poſſibly, then ſtrain it off, and pour it into the Veſſel, it will foon be fine but you may add two or three Quarts of Sack, or white Wine to fine it, Raiſins of the Sun will do as well as Malaga Raiſins if they cannot be had.

To make Elder Wine, very excellent.

Take Malago Raiſins, cut them ſmall, Stalks, Stones and all, put them into a Tub, pour over them Water that has boil'd an Hour, to every fix Pounds
of

of Raisins put one Gallon of Water, pour it on boiling hot and stir it well, and when it is cold cover it with a Cloth, and let it work together ten or twelve Days, stiring it five or six Times a Day. at the End of that Time strain the Liquor from the Raisins and squeeze them hard, put to every Gallon of Liquor one Pint of clear Juice of Elder. The best Way to get the Juice is to bake the Berries in earthen Pots, let the Liquor be cold when you put them together, and stir them well, then tun it, and when it has done working, clay it up and let it stand four or five Months before you bottle it; in six Weeks after it will be very ripe and fit for Use.

To make White Mead.

To every Gallon of Water put a Pint of Honey, and Half a Pound of Loaf Sugar, stir in the Whites of four Eggs beat to a Froth, and boil it as long as any Scum will arise, when it is cold work it with Yeast, and to every Gallon put the Juice and Peel of a large Lemon, stop it up when it has done working, and bottle it in ten Days.

Raisin Wine.

Put five Pounds of Malaga or Belvidere Raisins to a Gallon of clear River Water, steep them a Fortnight, stirring them every Day, then pour the Liquor off; squeeze the Juice out of the Raisins, and put both the Liquors together in a Vessel that is just large enough to contain it, for it should be quite full; let the Vessel stand till your Wine has

has done hissing, or making the usual Noise, you may add a Pint of French Brandy, to every two Gallons, then stop it close, and when you find it is Fine, which you may know by pegging it, bottle it off.

If you chuse to have it Red, put a Gallon of Alient Wine to every four Gallons of Raisin Wine.

Black Cherry Wine.

Take three Gallons of Water, boil it an Hour bruise twelve Pounds of Black Cherries, but do not break the Stones, pour the Water boiling hot on the Cherries, stir the Cherries very well in it, let it stand for 24 Hours, then strain it off, and to every Gallon put near two Pound of good Sugar, mix it well with the Liquor and let it stand 24 Hours longer, then put it in a clean sweet Cask, and stop it close, don't bottle it before you find it to be very fine.

To make Currant Wine.

Take your Currants full ripe, strip 'em and bruise them in a Mortar, and to every Gallon of Pulp put two Quarts of Water, first boiled and cold, you may put in some Rapes if you please, let it stand in a Tub to ferment, then let it run through a Hair Sieve: Let no Person touch it and let it take its Time to run, and to every Gallon of this Liquor put two Pounds and a Half of White Sugar, stir it well and put it in your Vessel, and to every six Gallons

lons put in a quart of the beſt rectified Spirits of Wine, let it ſtand ſix Weeks and bottle it.

Damſon Wine.

To every Gallon of Water put two Pounds and a half of Sugar, which you muſt boil and ſcum it three quarters of an Hour, and to every Gallon put five Pints of Damſons ſtoned, let them boil till it is of a fine Colour, then ſtrain it through a fine ſieve work it in an open Veſſel three or four Days, then pour it off the Lees, and let it work in that Veſſel as long as it will, then ſtop it up for ſix or eight Months, then if fine you may bottle it, and keep it a Year or two in Bottles.

Raſberry Wine.

Take ripe Raſberries, bruiſe them with the back of a Spoon, ſtrain them and fill a Bottle with the Juice; ſtop it, but not very cloſe, let it by four or five Days: Then pour it off from the dregs, and add thereto as much Rheniſh or White-wine, as the Juice will well colour, that done ſweeten your Wine with loaf Sugar, and then you may bottle it for Uſe.

Another Way.

To every Quart of Fruit you muſt put boiling hot a Quart of Water, cover it very cloſe and let it ſtand 24 Hours, then ſtrain it, and to three Quarts of Liquor put two Pounds of good Sugar, ſtir it together and ſpread a Toaſt with Yeaſt, ſet it to work, and pour it off the Lees, put it into your

Veſſel,

Vessel, and when it has quite done working stop it up: If it is fine in six or seven Months you may bottle it, and keep it a Year in the Bottles.

☞ You must at first watch all Wines, and if you find them fret, then you must continue to Fine them off the Lees every Day for some time, as fast as any settles.

To fine Wine the Lisbon Way.

To every twenty Gallons of Wine, take the Whites of ten Eggs, a small handfull of Salt, beat it to a Froth, and mix it well with a Quart or more of the Wine, then pour it into the Vessel and in a few Days it will be fine.

To Clear Wine.

Take half a Pound of Hartshorn and dissolve it in Cyder, if it be for Cyder, Rhenish Wine, or for any other Liquor; this is enough for a Hogshead.

To recover Wine if turned sharp.

Rack off your Wine into another Vessel, and to ten Gallons put the following Powder, take Oyster Shells, scrape and wash off the brown dirty outside of the Shells, then dry them in an Oven till they will powder. A Pound of this Powder to every nine or ten Gallons of Wine, stir it well together, stop it up and let it stand to settle two or three Days, or till it is fine, then bottle it off and Cork it well.

To make Cyder.

Pull your Fruit before it is too ripe, and let it lie a Day or two to have a good sweat, your Apples must be Pippins. Pearmains, or Harvey (if you mix your Winter and Summer Fruit together it is never good) grind your Apples and press them and when your Fruit is all pressed, put it immediately into a Hogshead, where it may have room to work, but not vent, a little hole between the Hoops, and bung it close; put three or four Pounds of Raisons in the Hogshead and two Pounds of Sugar, it will make it work better; often racking it off is the Way to fine it and always rack it in small Vessels, keeping them close bunged, and only a small vent hole; if it should work after racking, put into the Vessel some Raisons for it to feed on and bottle it in March.

To keep Gooseberries, Damsons, Bullace, Plumbs, and Cherries in Bottles.

Take Goosberries green, the other Sorts before they be too ripe, put them in wide mouth'd Bottles, set them in a gentle Oven till the skin change colour. When cold, cork them down tight, and melt some Rosin on the top.

RULES for going to MARKET, and chusing FLESH.

BEEF.

THE right Ox Beef is best, and that which is so has a fine open grain: If young a kind of an oily smoothness, and if dinted with your Finger will immediately rise again; but if old will be rough and spungy, and the dent remain. Cow Beef is less boned than that of the Ox, the Flesh closer grained, the Lean of it somewhat paler, and the Fat whiter, but if young, the dent you make will rise again. Bull Beef is closer grained than either, much coarser, and if you pinch it feels rough: The Fat is hard and skinny, and has a Raukness in the scent.

For chusing Mutton.

To know when Mutton is young, the Flesh will pinch tender, and the Fat part easily from the Lean; but if old, the one will wrinkle, and remain so for some time, and the other not be pulled off easily, by reason of a number of small strings; Old Mutton may also be known when the Flesh shrinks from the Bones, and the Skin is loose: In Ewe Mutton the Flesh is of a paler Colour than the Weather, and of a closer grain. If there happens to be a rot among the Sheep, the Fat will be yellow, and the Flesh pale, loose from the one and

and if squeezed, a Dew like Sweat will rise upon it.

How to chuse Veal.

When the bloody Vein in the shoulder is blue, or a bright red, it is new, but if blackish, greenish or yellowish, then it is stale. The loin first taints under the kidney, and the Flesh when stale, is soft and slimy,

The Breast and Neck taint first at the upper end, and you may perceive a dusty yellow, or greenish appearance; the sweet bread on the Breast will be clammy, otherwise it will be fresh and good.

The Leg when new is known by the stiffness of the Joints; if limber the Flesh is clammy, and has green or yellowish spots, it is stale. The head is known as the Lambs. The Flesh of a Bull-Calf is redder and firmer than that of a Cow-Calf and the Fat harder.

You cannot be too careful in examining the scent, for even what looks beautiful to the Eye will prove musty.

To chuse Lamb

House-Lamb when good is very fat and white, and the Lean of a pale colour. Grass Lamb is somewhat of a higher colour, but the Fat is white in a fore Quarter of either you must observe the Neck-Vein, if it looks of a fine light blue, it is fresh killed, but if greenish or yellow, it is stale. Smell under the Kidney of a hind Quarter, and try

try the Knuckle, if it be limber, and has a faint Scent, do not venture to buy it.

When you buy a Lamb's-Head, obferve the Eyes, if they are funk in and wrinkled it is ftale, if lively and plump it is new and fweet.

To chufe Pork.

If it be young and frefh the Flefh will be of a fine bright colour, but not too red, the Skin will be thin, and if you nip it with your Nails the Impreffion will remain, but if the Lean be high coloured, the Fat flabby, and the Rind hard, it is old.

For knowing whether it be new killed, try the Legs, Hands, and Springs, by putting you fingers under the Bone that comes out, fo if it be tainted you will there find it by fmelling your fingers; befides the Skin will be fweaty and clammy when ftale, but cool and fmooth when new.

How to chufe Vennifon.

Run a Knife under the bones that come out of the Haunches or Shoulders, and if the fcent is fweet, it is new, but if the fcent be rank, then it is ftale, and the fide in the moft flefhy part when tainted will look in fome places green, others very black. If the hoofs are wide and rough it is old, but if clofe and fmooth it is young.

Weftphalia or Englifh Hams.

Thefe are to be tried by putting a Knife under the Bone that flicks out, and if it comes out in a

manner

manner clean, and has a curious flavour, the Ham is sweet and good; if on the contrary, it is much smeared and sullied, and smells rank, the Ham was tainted before it was dried, or grown rusty afterwards.

To chuse Bacon.

When the Fat is white, oily in feeling, and does not break or crumble, and the Flesh sticks well to the Bones, and bears a good colour, it is good, but if the contrary, and the lean as some little streaks of yellow, it is rusty, or will soon be so.

Bacon may also be known if young by the thinness of the Rind. That Bacon which gives, and becomes flabby in wet Weather, is not well cured and will soon be rusty.

POULTRY.

How to know a Capon.

If a Capon be young, his Spurs are short and his Legs smooth, if a true Capon, a fat Vein on the side of the Breast, the Comb pale, and a thick Belly and Rump, if new a close hard Vent, if stale a loose open one.

A Cock and Hen.

If young, his Spurs are short and dubbed; but take Notice whether they are not pared or scraped by the seller, in order to deceive you. You may know if he is new by the Vent, in the same manner, as you judge of the Capon. and so also of a
Hen

Hen, but if young her Legs and Combare smooth if old they are rough.

Cock or Hen Turkey, or Turkey Poults.

If the Cock be young, his Legs will be black and smooth. and his Spurs short, if old, the contrary: if stale, his Eyes will be sunk, and his Feet dark and dry; and if new, the Eyes will look lively, and the Feet pliable. The like observation with respect to the Hen, but if she be with Egg, she will have an open Vent; if not, a hard close vent. Turkey Poults are known the same way, as to bring new or stale.

A Goose.

If the Bill of a Goose be Yellow, and she have but few Hairs, she is young; but if there are many, and the Bill and Feet red, she is old; if new, limber, if stale the contrary. A Goose that is not very fleshy on the Breast, and fat in the Rump, is not worth buying.

A Duck.

A Duck is to be judged in the same manner as a Goose,

Chickens.

Chuse the white-legged, for they are generally the best, and taste the sweetest.

A Wild Duck.

A right Wild Duck has a reddish Foot, and smaller than the Tame one, the marks of being young

young or old, new or stale, are the same as with the others.

A Woodcock or Snipe.

Chuse those that are thick, Fat, and the Flesh firm; the Nose dry, and the Throat clear, otherwise they are bad. Snipe. if young and fat, has a full Vein under the Wing, and feels thick in the Vent. As for the rest like the Woodcock.

A Partridge.

When the Bill is white, and the Legs blueish, it shews Age. for if young the Bill is black, and the Legs yellowish. Smell at their Mouths to know if they are new or stale.

Pigeons.

Old Pigeons have generally red Legs, and in some parts are blackish: If young and fresh the Flesh looks all of one colour, and are fat in the Vent. And thus of grey or green Plover, Fellfare, Black-birds, Thrush, Larks, and Wild Fowl in general.

A Hare.

A Hare is white and stiff when new and clean kill'd, if stale, the flesh will have a blackish Hue. If the Cleft in her Lip spread very much, and her Claws are wide and ragged, she is old, the contrary when young.

A Leverit.

To know a true Leverit, feel on the fore Leg near the Foot, and if there be a small Bone or knob it is right, if not, it is no Leverit but a Hare; and for the rest of the Marks, you may judge as of the Hare.

A Rabbit.

The Wild Rabbit is better than the Tame; and to destinguish the one from the other, you must observe the Head, which is more peaked in the Wild than the Tame. If it is old, there will be a great deal of yellowish Fat about the Kidneys, the Claws will be long, and the Wool rough and mottled with grey Hairs; if young the reverse. If stale, it will be limber and look bluish, having a kind of slime upon it, but if fresh it will be stiff and the flesh white and dry.

The best Instructions for chusing FISH.

ALL Sorts of Fish may be judged by the redness of their Gills, if no deceit be used, but as there is often an Imposition by wetting them with Blood, you must observe whether they are stiff, if their Eyes stand out and full, and there Fins and Tailes are not shrivelled, for if these Symptoms do not answer; they are stale, notwithstanding the redness of their Gills.

For

For chusing Plaise, Flounders, and Dabs.

When new they are stiff, their Eyes look full and lively: The thickest are always the best eating. As Plaise and Flounders will live a long time out of the Water, whoever buys them after they are dead, may find them sweet, but their substance will be so far spent that they will almost dissolve in the Water they are boiled in, and will neither give relish nor Nourishment to the Stomach. To distinguish Plaise from Flounders, the latter are somewhat thicker, of a darker brown, and have some small specks of Orange colour; the Plaise have spots too, but they are not so bright but longer. The best Sort are bluish on the Belly.

For chusing Pickled Salmon.

When it is new and good the Scales are stiff and shining: and the Flesh is oily to the Touch, and parts without crumbling.

Fresh Salmon.

You must examine the grain and colour as you do Butcher's Meat, if the one be fine and the other high florid, the Salmon is good, but if coarse and pale it is the contrary: When it is perfectly new a great quantity of Blood will issue from it when it is cut, and the Liver look very clear and almost transparent.

Whitings.

These are a Fish which if not extremely stiff when you buy them, will neither broil or boil.

For chusing Pickled Sturgeon.

When good and fine, the Veins and Gristle are of a blue colour, the skin limber, the Flesh white the Fat pleasant scented, and may be cut without crumbling.

For chusing Cod.

The best are those which are thick towards the Head, and their Flesh when cut is very white.

For chusing Soals.

The best are stiff and thick, and of a Cream colour on the Belly.

For chusing Red Herrings.

The best red Herrings are those that smell well and of a good gloss and part well from the Bone.

For chusing dried Lyng.

Observe that the best is thick about the pole, and its Flesh of a bright yellow.

For chusing Prawns and Shrimps.

These if stale will cast a slimy smell, their colour fading, and they slimy, otherwise all of them are good.

For chusing Crabs.

If stale they will be limber in their Claws and Joints, their red colour turned blackish and dusty, and will have a very bad smell under their Throats.

For chusing Lobsters.

The weightiest are the best, but take care there be no Water in them, and when fresh the Tail will fly up like a spring, and will be full of firm Flesh.

How to chuse Eggs.

The best Eggs are those which have a clear thin Shell, are of the longest Oval, and most peaked at the ends. Hold them before the Light, and if the White is clear, and the Yolk flows regularly in the midst; they are good, and the contrary when the White looks cloudy and the Yolk sinks which way soever you hold it. Or, hold the great end to your Tongue, when it feels warm it is new, if cold it is bad, and so in proportion to the heat and cold, so is the goodness of the Egg. Another Way to know a good Egg is to put the Egg in a Pan of cold Water, the fresher it be the sooner it will fall to the bottom, if rotten it will not sink at all.

How to keep Eggs good.

Put them all with the small end downwards in fine Wood ashes, turning them once a Week endways, and they will keep some Months.

How to chuse Butter.

When you buy Butter, run a knife in the middle of it, and if your smell and taste be good, you cannot be deceived.

How to chuse Cheese.

Chuse it by its moist and smooth Coat, if old Cheese it will be rough-coated, rugged or dry at top, beware of small Worms or Mites. If it be all over full of holes, moist or spungy, it is subject to Maggots. If any soft or perished place appear on the out-side, try how deep it goes, for the greater part may be hid within.

Observe how they are to be set on the Table.

SOOP Broth, or Fish, should always be set at the head of the Table; if none of these, a boiled Dish goes to the head, where there are both boiled and roasted.

If there be but one principle Dish it goes to the head of the Table.

If four, the biggest to the head, and next biggest to the Foot, and the two small Dishes on the sides.

If three, the two small ones to stand opposite nigh the Foot.

If five you are to put the smallest in the middle, the other four opposite.

If six, you are to put the top and bottom as before, the four small ones opposite for side Dishes.

Observe, though I have called all these Dishes, they are many of them, especially side Dishes, only Sauce, Gravy, Pickles, Sallad, or Greens answerable anfwerable to the feafon of the Year, or nature of the Meat for Inftance.

To boiled Beef, Cabbage or Sprouts, and Carrots with fome Butter,

To boiled Mutton, Turnips and Capers mixed a little Butter,

To a Leg of Pork, Turnips and Peas Pudding.

To boiled Veal, Bacon and Greens,

To boiled Fowls and Bacon, Cabbage or Sprouts and Carrots,

To boiled Fowls if not Bacon, Liver-fauce,

To roafted Fowls, good Gravy-fauce; Saufages fried for garnifh.

To roafted Beef, Mutton, or Veal, Horfe-raddifh, Sallad, Potatoes, or Pickles,

To roafted Lamb, Mint-fauce chop'd, with Sugar and Vinegar,

To roafted Pork, or Goofe, Apple-fauce and Muftard.

To falt Fifh, Parfnips and Eggs, boiled hard, minc'd and mix'd with Butter,

To roafted Rabbits, Liver-fauce and a little Parfley chop'd together,

To boiled Rabbits, Onion-fauce boiled and buttered.

Rules to be obſeved in Dreſſing Proviſions.

YOU muſt obſerve as a genereal Rule, to put all ſalt Meat in cold Water, and freſh Meat into the Pot when boiling, and put Salt into the Water where freſh Fiſh or Greens are to be boiled. A large Buttock of Beef ſalted ſhould be waſhed and ſoaked ſome Hours before you put it into the Pot; Bacon the ſame: and a Ham ſhould be laid in ſoak over-night.

Now ſuppoſing Dinner is to be got ready againſt a certain time, and you have any of the following Diſhes to dreſs, take care your Fire is in good order, and put them into the Pot, or on the Spit, according to the time they will take up as follows.

Diſhes that require a quarter of an Hour Roaſting;
Patridges roaſted,
Pigeons roaſted.

Joints that require Half an Hour dreſſing;
Leg of Lamb boiled, of five Pounds,
A ſmall Fowl, or a Chicken, roaſted or boiled,
A Rabbit roaſted,
Pigeons boiled

Dishes that require Three Quarters of an Hour.
A large Fowl roasted.
Ditto boiled.
A Rabbit boiled.
N. B. A Pig roasted takes a full Hour.

Dishes requiring an Hour and a Quarter.
A Goose.
A Turkey boiled.

Joints requiring an Hour and a Half.
A Neck of Mutton boiled of seven Pounds.
A Neck of Veal roasted.
A Breast of Veal roasted of ten Pounds.
A Neck of Veal boiled of nine Pounds.
A Leg of Lamb boiled of nine Pounds.
A Hare roasted.
A Turkey.

Joints requiring Two Hours.
Leg of Mutton boiled of eight Pounds.
Shoulder of Mutton roasted of ten Pounds.
Leg of Mutton roasted of ten Pounds.
A Chine roasted of twelve Pounds.
A Loin of Veal roasted of eleven Pounds.
A Knuckle of Veal boiled of six Pounds.
A Loin of Pork roasted of eleven Pounds,
A leg of Pork boiled of ten Pounds.

Joints requiring Three Hours.
Brisket of Beef of fourteen Pounds.
Achbone of twenty-four Pounds

Chump End of a Sirloin roasted, of twenty four Pounds.

A Rib Piece, of twenty-four Pounds.

A Fillet of Veal roasted, of twelve Pounds.

☞ Rump of Beef roasted, of about eighteen Pounds, requires three Hours and a Half. And a Buttock of Beef, of twenty-four Pounds, takes full four Hours. Also a Ham of sixteen or twenty Pounds.

I shall next set down the different Names of the Joints of Meat, &c. For a Help to you when sent to Market, as Strangers are often apt to forget or mistake them.

BEEF.

An Ox Cheek is Half the Head.

The Shin is cut off the veiny Knuckle of the fore Quarter.

Ribs of Beef are cut off the fore Quarter.

The Sirloin is cut off the Chine Part of the hind Quarter.

Rump of Beef is cut off the Chine, and joins to the Sirloin.

Buttock of Beef is the thick Piece off the upper Part of the Thigh.

The Ach-bone joins to the Buttock.

The thick Flank comes off one side the Buttock.

Brisket comes off the Belly Part of the Ribs.

Veiny Piece is off the veiny Part of the thick Flank.

Thin

Thin Flank is the Belly Piece from the Brisket, and comes off the thin Part of the thick Flank and veiny Piece.

Mouse Buttock is a Piece cut from between the Buttock and Leg.

BACON.

Hock of Bacon is cut off the hind or fore Leg. The Best is the thin or Belly End of the Ribs.

MUTTON.

The Head with the Heart, Liver and Lights.

A Shoulder is the fore Leg cut from the fore Quarter.

A Neck, the fore Quarter next after the Shoulder is cut from it.

A Breast; the Belly End of the Ribs cut from the Neck.

A Leg cut from the hind Quarter.

A Loin, the hind Quarter after the Leg is cut from it.

A Chine is the two Loins not seperated.

N. B. Lamb comes under the same Names, only the Neck and Breast being commonly together, are called a Coast or Ribs of Lamb.

PORK.

Leg of Pork is the hind Leg cut from the Loin.

Spring of Pork is the fore Leg.

A fore Loin is cut off from the Spring.

A hind Loin is cut from the Hind Quarter after the Leg is cut from it.

Z 2   VEAL.

VEAL.

A Calves Head.
Shoulder of Veal is the fore Leg cut from the Neck and Breaſt.
Neck of Veal is the Ribs of the ſame Quarter.
Breaſt of Veal is the Belly Part of the Ribs from the Neck.
Leg of Veal is the Leg cut whole from the Loin,
Fillet of Veal is the Leg when the Knuckle is cut off.
Knuckle of Veal is cut off from the Fillet.
Loin of Veal is the hind Quarter cut from off the Leg.

POULTRY.

A Turkey. A Fowl. A Pullet. A Capon. A Chicken. A Rabbit. A Hare. A Partridge. A Woodcock. Larks. A Gooſe. A Duck. Gooſe Giblets. A Pidgeon. A Wood Pidgeon.

HERBS.

Parſley, Thyme, Onions, Sage, Aſparagus, Turnips, Parſnips, Carrots, Savoys, Sprouts, Caulliflowers, Potatoes, Cellery, Beet Roots, Pot Herbs, Peas, Beans, Spinage, Sallad, Cucumbers, Artichokes, Endive.

The London and Country BREWER,

CARE muſt be taken to have the Malt clean; and let it ſtand a Week after being ground, before you uſe it.

Thirteen Buſhels of Malt will make a Hogſhead of exceeding ſtrong Beer, Hops eight Pounds; it will afterwards make near a Hogſhead of Small Beer, with one Pound and a Half of freſh Hops to it.

Eight Buſhels of Malt will make a Hogſhead of excellent Ale, and the like Quantity of ſmall Beer, in making the Ale five Pound of Hops; for ſmall Beer (after) add one Pound and a Half of Hops.

It may generally be obſerved, where Ale is deſigned for keeping, that a Pound of Hops ſhould be allowed to every Buſhel of Malt; if deſigned for preſent ſpending, little more than Half the Quantity will ſerve, tho' the Palate of the Perſon it is brew'd for ſhould be conſulted.

Take particular Care to have your Caſks, &c. well clean'd and dry'd, and never uſe them on any Occaſion but Wine-making or Brewing, it is a good Way to take out their Heads, and after being well cleaned with a Hand-bruſh, Sand, &c. put them in again, ſcald them well, throw into each Barrel, a Piece of unſlac'd Lime and ſtop in the Bung cloſe.

Having got your Caſks, &c. in readineſs, proceed as follows, &c. When you have a Copper of boiling Water ready, pour it into your Maſh Tub, and let it be cool enough to ſee your Face in, then pour in your Malt, and let it be well mashed, have a Copper of Water boiling in the mean Time, and when your Malt is well mashed fill your Mashing Tub, stir it well again and cover it over with a Sack. Let it stand three Hours, then set a broad shallow Tub under the Cock, let it run very softly, and if it is thick throw it up again till it runs fine, then throw in a Handful of Hops under the Tub, and let the Mash run into it and fill your Tub till it is all run off.

Have Water boiling in the Copper, and lay as much more as you have Occasion for, allowing one Third for boiling and waste, let that stand an Hour, boiling more Water to fill the Mash Tub for Small Beer, let the Fire down a litle, and put into the Tubs enough to fill your Mash.

Let the second Mash be run off, and fill your Copper with the first Wort, put in Part of your Hops and make it boil quick.

About an Hour is long enough; and when it is half boiled throw in a Handful of Salt.

Have a clean Stick and dip it into the Copper, and if the Wort feels clammy it is boiled enough.

Have ready a large Tub, put two Sticks acrofs, set your standing Basket over the Tub on the Sticks and strain your Wort thro' it.

Put your Wort on to boil with the rest of the Hops, Let your Mash be still cover'd with Water, and thin your Wort that is cooling in as many Things as you can, for the thinner it lies, and the quicker it cools the better.

When quite cold put it into the tunning Tub mind to throw a Handful of Salt into every Boil.

When the Mash has stood an Hour draw it off, then fill your Mash with cold Water, take off the Wort in the Copper and order it as before.

When cold, add to it the First in the Tub: So soon as you empty one Copper fill the other, to boil your Small Beer well.

Let the Mash run off, and when both are boiled with fresh Hops, order them as the two first Boilings; when cold empty the Mash Tub, and put the small Beer to work there.

When cool enough work it, set a wooden Bowl of Yeast in the Beer and it will work over, with some of the Beer in the Bowl.

Stir your Tun up every twelve Hours, let it stand two Days, then tun it, taking of the Yeast.

Fill your Vessels full, and save some to fill your Barrels, let it stand till it has done working, then lay on your Bung lightly for a Fortnight, after that stop it as close as you can.

Mind you have a Vent-peg at the Top of the Vessel, in warm Weather open it, and if your Drink hisses, as it often will, loosen it till it has done, then stop it close again.

If you can boil your Ale in one boiling, it is best if your Copper will admit of it: if not, boil it as Conveniency serves.

To sweeten very stinking or musty Casks.) Take and fill your Vessels with warm Water, and let it stand till the Yeast is well soak'd, then pour out your Water and put in more clean, and a few pebble Stones, then shake them about, which takes off the foul Yeast: But if any Scent remains, fill your Vessel fed with boiling Water, near, but not quite full, and directly put in Pieces of unflack'd Stone-lime, which will prefently fet the Water a boiling, that muſt ſtill be fed on with more Pieces, till the Ebullition has continued Half an Hour at leaſt, but if very bad, longer: And after you have ſo done, bung it down, and let it remain till it is almoſt cold and no longer, leaſt the Lime at the Bottom harden too much, and be difficult to waſh out.

To keep your Caſks from ſtinking.) When you have drawn off your Beer, bung them up cloſe with the Yeaſt in, and let them ſtand till the next Brewing, and that will keep them ſweet.

To cure a Hogſhead of four Ale or Beer.) Take four or five Pounds of lean Mutton cut in Pieces, four Ounces of Egg Shells dried, and Half an Ounce of Tartar, put theſe into the Caſk, and your Liquor will ſoon be reſtored to its firſt Perfection.

N. B. The above Quantity of Ingredients are for Half a Hogſhead of either Ale or Beer, if the Liquor be more in Quantity, the Ingredients muſt be increaſed in proportion thereto.

www.ingramcontent.com/pod-product-compliance
Lightning Source LLC
Chambersburg PA
CBHW032149160426
43197CB00008B/828